On Divorce

by
John MacArthur, Jr.

MOODY PRESS
CHICAGO

© 1983 by
JOHN F. MACARTHUR, JR.

Moody Press Edition, 1985

Original title: *Jesus' Teaching on Divorce*

Library of Congress Cataloging-in-Publication Data

MacArthur, John F.
   On Divorce

     (John MacArthur's Bible studies)
     Includes index.
     1   Divorce—Biblical teaching   2. Bible. N.T.
Matthew XIX, 1-12—Criticism, interpretation, etc.
3. Bible. N.T. Corinthians, 1st, VII—Criticism,
interpretation, etc. I. Title. II. Series: MacArthur,
John F. Bible studies.
BS2545.D58M33 1985   261.8'3589   85-26004

ISBN: 0-8024-5111-X

5 6 7 Printing/EP/Year 91 90 89 88

Contents

These Bible studies are taken from messages delivered by Pastor-Teacher John MacArthur, Jr., at Grace Community Church in Panorama City, California. The recorded messages themselves may be purchased as a series or individually. Please request the current price list by writing to:

WORD OF GRACE COMMUNICATIONS
P.O. Box 4000
Panorama City, CA 91412

Or call the following toll-free number:
1-800-55-GRACE

1
Jesus' Teaching on Divorce—
Part I

Outline

Introduction
A. The Subject of Divorce
   1. The alarming statistics
      a) Divorce: the numerical accounting
      b) Divorce: the nauseating approach
      c) Divorce: the nonchalant attitude
   2. The alternative stance
   3. The accommodated standard
      a) The standard raised
      b) The standard lowered
B. The Setting for Jesus' Teaching
   1. The ministry in Galilee ended
   2. The message on the childlikeness of the believer concluded
      a) The Sermon on the Mount
      b) The discourse on discipleship
      c) The parables of the kingdom
      d) The Olivet discourse
   3. The ministry in Perea begun
      a) The region of Perea
      b) The residents of Perea
      c) The route to Jerusalem
   4. The multitudes of Perea following

Lesson
I. The Attack
   A. The Pharisees' Attempt to Discredit Jesus
      1. The pertinent data
         a) The Pharisees' view of divorce
         b) Jesus' view of divorce
      2. The plan
   B. The Pharisees' Attempt to Destroy Jesus
      1. The imprisonment of John the Baptist
         a) The region of his imprisonment
         b) The reason for his imprisonment
      2. The implications of Jesus' view of divorce
II. The Answer
   A. God's Law Against Divorce Reiterated
      1. One man for one woman

     a) The intention
     b) The inadvisability
     c) The impossibility
  2. A strong bond
     a) The Hebrew idea of cleaving
     b) The Hebrew word for marriage
  3. One flesh
  4. A work of God
     a) The passage misused
     b) The point compared

Introduction

A. The Subject of Divorce

  1. The alarming statistics

In *Newsweek* magazine a journalist asked a rather simple yet profound question. He said, "Is there anyone left in the land who has not heard a friend, a child, or a parent describe the agony of divorce?" (Jan. 10, 1983, p. 42). The answer to that question is, "No!"

    a) Divorce: the numerical accounting

Divorce has not only become epidemic, it's become pandemic. All of us are touched by it either in our own families or in our circle of friends. In the United States in 1982 there were over one million divorces. In 1983 there were at least a million more. Beneath the rubble of those numbing statistics lie the crushed lives of men, women, and children. For every one million divorces there are two million spouses and maybe two to three million children. Possibly five to six million people a year are being impacted by divorce—and it goes on year after year. Divorce is a staggering problem. In fact, forty-eight out of the fifty states have "no-fault" laws that make divorce as easy as getting a marriage license without a blood test!

What held marriages together in the past?

In the past, families and marriages were held together for the most part. Divorce is a relatively new phenomenon. The divorce rate in America has doubled in the last twenty years and threatens to do so again in the next twenty years. But in the past, marriages mostly held together. I think there were three reasons for this.

1. Family moral force—In the past, a person's family meant something. Mom, dad, husband, wife, children, uncles, aunts, brothers, and sisters were each specially important. Life used to revolve around the family. The love, care, hope, and comfort that were found in the family provided needed security. Then families began to fly apart because of such factors as the

invasion of television, working mothers, the mobility of our society, the automobile, and so on. And once the family began to disintegrate, there was no longer a cohesive unit that forced a moral value system on its members.

2. Community expectation

   A second factor that used to hold marriages together was community expectation or peer pressure. As recently as twenty-five years ago, divorce was often seen as a scandal. There used to be a certain amount of pressure holding marriages together that was applied by the expectations of a community that valued marriage. Today those traditions have basically been abandoned.

3. Church doctrine

   Perhaps the most powerful of all the forces that held marriage together in the past was church doctrine. However, that too has been conveniently jettisoned. There has been such an emasculating of the biblical statements about divorce that the church has acquiesced to the demands of a constituency that is pleading for more and more concessions all the time. So divorce, even in the church, has become a staggering reality.

The family and the community can't hold a marriage together anymore. And it seems the church is losing its influence, too, as it abandons the biblical standard.

b) Divorce: the nauseating approach

The nation's attitude about divorce was summed up in an ad I saw in a local paper not long ago. It was in a little box in a very visible place in the paper, and it read like this: "Divorce—$25. Divorce Centers of California. Unload that turkey!" That gives you a little idea of how far our society has gone, doesn't it?

c) Divorce: the nonchalant attitude

A well-known woman who appears on television and claims to be a born-again Christian represents the attitude of many people—even people in the church. She is divorcing her husband to pursue her career. She says, "I'm happier than I was before the divorce because I'm my own person, making decisions on my own." She doesn't believe that divorce affects her religious beliefs in any significant way. She says, "In my mind, God is a forgiving father and He loves me despite the divorce. I'm hoping I'm not judged as a Christian on the basis of a divorce. Chuck and I are both happier being divorced friends than married enemies" (*Pittsburgh Press*, May 30, 1982).

It all sounds so nice, but we are forced to recognize and deal with the very disturbing fact that the sacred bond of marriage is being ruptured at an incredible rate. Even the church is not

3

immune to this. It has caught the world's perspective more than it should have and has emasculated the biblical doctrine of marriage.

2. The alternative stance

   As Christians, we have two choices. We can either listen to the world's opinion or to the Lord's Word. Those are the only two choices. Either we go with the flow of society and give in to their system or we hold up the Word of God and say, "This is what God requires. As for me and my house, we will hear the Word of the Lord."

3. The accommodated standard

   You say, "John, there seems to be an awful lot of confusion over what the Bible teaches about divorce. So how can we know just what God's standard is?" I'm amazed, frankly, that there is so much discrepancy. I think the Bible is very clear about what it says about divorce and remarriage. In fact, it's as clear as it's ever going to get, because it has been saying the same thing ever since it was written. I don't think the problem is that the Bible is unclear, I think the problem is fuzzy thinking. And what fuzzes up people's thinking is that they go to the Bible with certain preconceptions and consequently change its standard.

   a) The standard raised

   Some people look at the divorce rate and say, "We have to stop divorce!" So in order to stop divorce, they come up with a doctrine that says, "No divorce for anybody, for any reason, and absolutely no remarriage for anyone, anytime, for anything." Now, that sounds like a very good standard. In fact, I wish I could believe it. Why? Because it would end a lot of counseling problems. We could just say, "All divorce is wrong. Period." There would be no remarriage, and we wouldn't have to counsel people in that area. It would be nice if it was that airtight, but we can't do that. We can't look at the problem in the world and say, "In order to stop the problem, let's take the Bible's standard and raise it." That's not right.

   b) The standard lowered

   On the other hand, there are those who look at the problem of divorce and say, "We have to minister to these people, care for these people, love these people, and accept these people. So let's lower the standard to accommodate everybody. After all, we don't want to put any undue pressure on them. Basically we want them all to be happy, so we'll just tell them to work it out the best way they can. The Lord will forgive them."

   So, on the one hand are the people who want to raise the standard, and on the other hand are the people who want to lower the standard. But what we must do is go back and see what is recorded in the pages of Scripture. And we're going to do that as we study Matthew 19:1–12.

Before we look at Jesus' teaching on divorce in verses 3–12, we must first examine verses 1 and 2.

B. The Setting for Jesus' Teaching

Look for a moment at Matthew 19:1–2. "And it came to pass that, when Jesus had finished these sayings, he departed from Galilee, and came into the borders of Judea beyond the Jordan. And great multitudes followed him, and he healed them there." Now this is a very important passage, but most people probably skim right by it to get to verses 3–12. However, these two verses are very important because they mark a significant transition in the life of our Lord.

1. The ministry in Galilee ended (v. 1*b*)

"He departed from Galilee."

This spells out the end of the Galilean ministry—a monumental moment in the life of our Lord. Since Matthew 4:12, when the Lord began His Galilean ministry, He had been ministering, preaching, teaching, and healing—bringing light to "Galilee of the Gentiles" (Matt. 4:15*b*–16). But as always, "Men loved darkness rather than light" (John 3:19*b*). As long as the light was there, the majority of the population never really came to the light. Now the Galilean ministry was over, the light went out, and after approximately two years of ministry in that one area, Jesus turned from Galilee in the north to go south to Jerusalem. Entering into the last phase of His life, our Lord began to move toward the cross, His passion, and His resurrection.

So, the little statement "he departed from Galilee" is extremely important because it marks the end of His Galilean ministry. The people had their opportunity, their day in the sun, their moment of truth. But now it ends.

2. The message on the childlikeness of the believer concluded (v. 1*a*)

"And it came to pass that, when Jesus had finished these sayings."

The "sayings" of verse 1 refer back to Jesus' discourse in chapter 18 on the childlikeness of the believer. Matthew contains many such discourses, sermons, or lessons. In chapter 18, Jesus was in a home in Capernaum with a little infant on His lap. Using that infant as an illustration, He taught a great discourse on the childlikeness of the believer. Now 19:1 says, "And it came to pass that, when Jesus had finished these sayings." This statement is very interesting, because it pops up several times in Matthew at the conclusion of major discourses. It's as if this phrase is used to sign off the major discourses.

5

a) The Sermon on the Mount—This first major discourse in Matthew, from chapters 5-7, ends in 7:28 with the following statement, "And it came to pass, when Jesus had ended these sayings."

b) The discourse on discipleship—The next great discourse in Matthew is in chapter 10, where the Lord teaches the apostles about discipleship. Chapter 11 begins similarly, "And it came to pass, when Jesus had ceased commanding his twelve disciples" (v. 1*a*).

c) The parables of the kingdom—Matthew 13 contains the great discourse on the parables of the kingdom. It ends in 13:53 with the statement, "And it came to pass that, when Jesus had finished these parables."

d) The Olivet discourse—The great prophetic discourse in Matthew 24-25 given on the Mount of Olives to the disciples ends in 26:1 with the following statement, "And it came to pass that, when Jesus had finished all these sayings."

This statement in Matthew 19:1 is a very important signature used by Matthew to point out that the Lord has just concluded a great discourse, a great sermon, a great lesson of significance.

3. The ministry in Perea begun (v. 1*c*)

"And came into the borders of Judea beyond the Jordan."

a) The region of Perea

The land of Palestine is split down the middle by the Jordan River, which runs from the Sea of Galilee in the north to the Dead Sea in the south. Galilee, in the north, is a rural area, while Judea, in the south, is the most populated area with Jerusalem as its major city.

Here in Matthew 19, the Lord is leaving Galilee to go to Jerusalem. But instead of going straight south to Judea, He will go east, cross the Jordan River, travel south along the eastern side of the Jordan, cross back over the Jordan in the south near Jericho, and then ascend the mountain to Jerusalem.

This route takes Jesus into a very interesting region—a region called "The Beyond" by the Jews. Why? Because it was the region beyond the Jordan. The term in the Greek is *peran*, from which we get the name *Perea* (lit., "the beyond"). So from His Galilean ministry, Jesus moves into His Perean ministry, which is discussed in Matthew 19-20.

b) The residents of Perea

In years past, Perea had been rather sparsely populated, but during the reign of Herod the Great, the Jewish population of Perea had greatly increased. Also at this time, Perea was under the control of Herod Antipas, who had had John the Baptist beheaded. So the Lord, having ministered in Galilee, went east to the region beyond the Jordan to minister in Perea to the many Jews that had taken up residence there.

c) The route to Jerusalem

Any Jew traveling from Galilee in the north to Judea in the south would always cross over the Jordan and go down through Perea. You say, "Why didn't they just go straight south through Samaria?" Well, the Jews wouldn't travel through Samaria because they viewed the Samaritans as defiled and dangerous people.

As Jesus began His Perean ministry, it was close to the Passover and feast season, so there were many Jews on this same route to Jerusalem in the region of Perea. The Lord then would be able to minister to the inhabitants of Perea as well as to the pilgrims on their way to Jerusalem.

4. The multitudes of Perea following (v. 2)

"And great multitudes followed him, and he healed them there."

These healings were the manifestation of Jesus' messianic credentials as well as the revelation of His power and compassion. In Mark 10:1, which is a parallel passage, it says that He taught the multitudes as well. So His ministry in Perea was very much like His Galilean ministry. A crowd would gather, and He would teach and heal them—giving them the Word of God and affirming its truthfulness (Himself as the spokesman of God) by His miraculous compassion and power. As He moved toward the cross and His own death, He was still consumed with the needs of the people, teaching the truth of God, and bringing the people to an understanding that He was, in fact, the Messiah.

As Jesus moves along with the crowd of verse 2, verse 3 tells us that His steps were dogged by the Pharisees. They wouldn't leave Him alone. They were His archenemies—incessantly hatching sinister plots to discredit Him and take His life. The Pharisees, who represented the religious establishment, were constantly being unmasked by virtue of the truth that Jesus was preaching. Consequently, they hated Him, despised Him, and wanted to do everything they could to eliminate Him.

As we come to verse 3, we meet the Pharisees and the first point in our outline.

Lesson

I. THE ATTACK (v. 3)

"The Pharisees also came unto him, testing him, and saying unto him, Is it lawful for a man to put away his wife for every cause?"

The Pharisees wanted to bring Jesus a test He couldn't pass. They had two objectives in mind. First, they wanted to discredit Him with the people so that He would lose His popularity. Second, they wanted to destroy Him. Now the question they asked is not some whimsical question fired off the tops of their heads—it is calculated, studied, and

7

planned out. On the surface it might seem like a rather innocent question, but they had thought this thing through. It is a clever, wilely, sinister, astute question—meant to attack Jesus Christ by discrediting and destroying Him.

A. The Pharisees' Attempt to Discredit Jesus

1. The pertinent data

    a) The Pharisees' view of divorce

Divorce was a volatile issue among the Jews. The Old Testament standard had been lowered to make divorce easy, so the practice became very, very common. The Pharisees were leaders in this, not only by what they taught, but by their example. They were continually divorcing their wives and teaching that it could be done for any reason at all. In fact, this doctrine was very popular among the people as well, especially among those who wanted to get a divorce. Actually, it merely accommodated the sinners at the level of their sin.

There had been a reigning rabbinical feud between Rabbi Shammai, who said that there was to be no divorce, and Rabbi Hillel, who said that you could divorce your wife for any reason at all. Rabbi Shammai didn't have a great following because his view wasn't popular with the people. But Rabbi Hillel, who had died just twenty years before Christ's ministry, still had the dominant, popular view. He taught that you could divorce your wife for burning the dinner, for putting too much salt on your food, for spinning around in the street so that someone saw her knees, for taking her hair down, for speaking to men, or for saying something unkind about her mother-in-law. You could even divorce her if you found someone prettier, because then she became unclean in your sight. You could divorce her if she was infertile or if she didn't give you a male child. In other words, you could divorce your wife for any reason at all. This was the popular view—and the view the Pharisees taught.

    b) Jesus' view of divorce

The Pharisees knew that Jesus didn't agree with their view of divorce. In a confrontation with them in Matthew 5:27–32, He basically says, "You say you don't commit adultery, but you're the worst kind of adulterers. You proliferate adultery all over the place because you divorce without cause. The person you divorce becomes an adulterer when she remarries and makes an adulterer of the one she marries. Also, when you remarry, you become an adulterer and make an adulterer of the one you marry. You're causing adultery all over the place because you divorce without cause."

So the Pharisees knew that Jesus took a firm line on divorce—a view that wasn't popular. In fact, Jesus' view of divorce given in Matthew 5:31–32 and Luke 16:18 must have traveled like wildfire because of the high interest in that particular issue.

2. The plan

What the Pharisees are hoping here in Matthew 19:3 is that Jesus will come out with a strong, overt statement on divorce and alienate and intimidate all the people who are divorced. They want Him to say, "You're a bunch of fornicating adulterers," so that they can trap Him into such a narrow-minded, rigid, hardline viewpoint that His popularity will be destroyed. And not only do they want to show Jesus as being intolerant, they also want to show Him as being uncommitted to the great teachings of the rabbis and Pharisees. In other words, they're hoping they can discredit Him by forcing Him into a corner as some kind of hard-bound, hard-nosed legalist—against the popular view. They wanted Him to blurt something out that would cause the people to reject Him and walk away.

Not only did the Pharisees want to discredit Jesus, they had another sinister motive in asking Jesus the question of verse 3.

B. The Pharisees' Attempt to Destroy Jesus

The Pharisees wanted Jesus dead. Even if nobody believed what He said, He was still a problem to them. Why? Because of His intimidating confrontations of the errors in their life and doctrine. So they wanted to destroy Him. You say, "Well, how in the world could this destroy Him?" Let me show you.

1. The imprisonment of John the Baptist

   a) The region of his imprisonment

   We don't know much about Perea, but we do know the following. We know there was a city called "Bethany beyond the Jordan" (John 1:28, NASB*) in Perea, where John the Baptist was baptizing. We also know that when Herod Antipas had John imprisoned, it was at his palace in Perea called Machaerus.

   You say, "Is that important?" Yes, it is.

   b) The reason for his imprisonment

   Look at Matthew 14:3: "For Herod [Herod Antipas, who ruled that area] had laid hold on John, and bound him, and put him in prison." Why? "For [or 'because of'] Herodias' sake, his brother Philip's wife." Now, that's a very important statement. Do you know who Herodias was? She was the wife of Herod Antipas. You say, "Well, why does the Bible call her 'his brother Philip's wife'?" Because she was Philip's wife before Herod Antipas seduced her and stole her away from his own brother. Notice, however, that God does

*New American Standard Bible.

not recognize this adulterous union and call it marriage. The reason the Bible still refers to Herodias as "his brother Philip's wife" is that in the eyes of God that's the way it still was.

As a footnote, not only was Herodias his own brother's wife, she was also his blood relative (the daughter of Herod Antipas's half brother, Aristobulus). So Herod Antipas had an incestuous, adulterous union—which the Word of God did not recognize as a legitimate marriage.

You say, "Well, what does all of this have to do with Jesus answering the Pharisees' question about divorce?" Look at verse 4 of Matthew 14. Here we see why John was thrown into prison. "For John said unto him [Herod Antipas], It is not lawful for thee to have her [Herodias]." You see, John was put into prison because he spoke up about God's law on divorce. In fact, ultimately he had his head chopped off because he confronted this evil man and his evil partner with the fact that their marriage was not lawful before God.

2. The implications of Jesus' view of divorce

"If it cost John the Baptist his life to confront Herod with his view of divorce," thought the Pharisees, "then if Jesus voices this same view in the region of Herod Antipas's jurisdiction, maybe He'll get His head chopped off too!" Do you understand their logic? I believe the Pharisees were hoping to have Jesus publicly pronounce the reigning monarch of the area as a fornicating adulterer, and thus put His life in jeopardy.

So the Pharisees' question about divorce in verse 3 is not just some whimsical question. They wanted to discredit Him with the people and destroy Him. It was a sinister attack!

I want you to notice His response. It is so profound and astute that it's staggering. He evades them so marvelously that it's utter genius.

II. THE ANSWER (vv. 4–6)

"And he answered and said unto them, Have ye not read that he who made them at the beginning, made them male and female; and said, For this cause shall a man leave father and mother, and shall cleave to his wife, and they two shall be one flesh? Wherefore, they are no more two, but one flesh. What, therefore, God hath joined together, let no man put asunder [or 'divorce']."

A. God's Law Against Divorce Reiterated

Jesus didn't answer the Pharisees' question immediately from His own authority. He initially went beyond Himself, beyond their customs, beyond their rabbis, and beyond their traditions, all the way back to what God says in the very beginning in Genesis 1:27 and 2:24. In other words, He says, "Your argument isn't with Me, it's with God. So let me quote God on this subject, because God's Word is the foundation of this issue."

10

It's also interesting to note Jesus' sarcasm when He said to these men who spent all of their time reading and interpreting the Bible, "Have ye not read?" Well, it's obvious that they had read Genesis 1:27 and 2:24, but Jesus was pointing out their utter ignorance. What a slap at their religious pride and their boasted knowledge of the law. "You who are so clever, who possess, maintain, and interpret the Law, have you not read what it says—even at the very beginning?"

As Jesus quoted from God out of Genesis, He gave four reasons why it is not lawful to divorce for any cause—reiterating God's law against divorce.

1. One man for one woman (v. 4)

"Have ye not read that he who made [lit., 'created'] them at the beginning, made them male and female?"

Jesus says, "Haven't you read about the creation, fellas? Haven't you gotten into that text yet? Do you remember what it says? It says that God made them a male and a female, right?"

a) The intention

When God created, He created Adam and He created Eve. That's it! He did not create spares. He didn't create Adam, Eve, and Ethel, or Adam, Eve, and Albert—just in case. He did not create eight people or nine people or seven people or thirteen people or three people, and say, "Look, if it doesn't work out, try somebody else." When God created, He created Adam and Eve—period! There were no spares, options, or alternatives. The divine intention in the very beginning was one man for one woman. He didn't make provision for polygamy or divorce by creating spare people. Now that seems like a rather obvious point.

b) The inadvisability

Divorce for Adam and Eve was not advisable. Not only would it have gotten very lonely in the Garden, but if they had divorced, Genesis would have ended in chapter 1, right? Divorce was not an option. That's the point of what Jesus is saying.

c) The impossibility

In the case of Adam and Eve, divorce was not only wrong and inadvisable, it was impossible. There were no alternatives—nowhere to go—no one else to talk to. But that's the way God meant it. If it wasn't those two, it wasn't anyone. God's intended creation was a non-optional, indissolvable union: one man for one woman.

When God created one man for one woman, He set that standard in motion for all of human history. Just because spares came along as time went on, it didn't change God's intention. God never intended for married people to be poking around to see if

11

they like somebody better. That's not an alternative God ever intended.

So divorce is not permitted by virtue of creation.

2. A strong bond (v. 5*a*)

"For this cause shall a man leave father and mother, and shall cleave to his wife."

Jesus moves from Genesis 1:27 to Genesis 2:24—still in the very primitive revelation of Scripture prior to the fall of man. God's perfect purpose and plan was for a man and woman to leave their parents and cleave to one another—breaking the family bond.

a) The Hebrew idea of cleaving

The word "cleave" basically means "to have a bond that can't be broken." It carries with it the idea of being glued or stuck. In fact, one Bible translation that I read translates Genesis 2:24 to say that a man should be glued to his wife.

Also inherent in the word "cleave" is the idea of pursuing hard after something. So the idea of cleaving, then, is two people stuck together because they pursue hard after each other—two hearts diligently and utterly committed to pursuing one another in love, stuck together in an indissolvable bond, and glued in mind, will, spirit, and emotion.

b) The Hebrew word for marriage

There is a beautiful remnant of the divine intention of marriage that finds itself in the Jewish language. The Hebrew word for marriage is *kiddushin*. Basically, *kiddushin* means "consecration" or "sanctification." To consecrate or sanctify something means "to set something apart to God." So, when a Jew said something was *kiddushin*, he meant that it had become the personal possession of God—totally surrendered to God. That same word is their word for marriage.

Marriage is a consecration of two people to each other. It is a consecration that says, "I am totally separated unto you." It is a union of two people whose utter devotion is to each other. In fact, according to 1 Corinthians 7:2–4, a husband and wife actually become the personal possession of one another.

Also inherent in the word *kiddushin* is the idea that not only is marriage a setting apart and a consecration to each other, it's a setting apart and consecration of that union to God. That's the purest perspective of marriage.

So God doesn't allow divorce because He created one man for one woman and because of the strong bond of an indissoluble union with no option.

12

3. One flesh (v. 5b–6a)

"And they two shall be one flesh? Wherefore, they are no more two, but one flesh."

You can't divide one. It is the indivisible number. In marriage, two people become one—there aren't two anymore. And when two people become one they are indivisible. You can't have half a person, because half a person is nobody at all! In the union of marriage, two become one person.

You say, "What does it mean to be one person?" Well, I think it is a divine perception. When two people come together, in God's view they literally become one person. They abandon themselves to each other, become the total possession of each other, and become one in mind, spirit, goals, direction, emotions, feeling, and will. And that oneness, ultimately, is best seen in the child they produce. That child is the perfect emblem of their union, because it bears all that the parents are, in one body.

You can't talk about breaking up two people in a marriage, because when a marriage is broken up, one person is sliced in half. Then what do you have? Two halves—and two halves are nobody.

Finally, there's a fourth reason why divorce is not God's desire. And perhaps this is the strongest of all biblical reasons.

4. A work of God (v 6b)

"What, therefore, God hath joined together, let no man put asunder."

The phrase "put asunder" is the Greek verb *chōrizō*. Literally it means "to divorce." In 1 Corinthians 7:11, *chōrizō* is used in the same way. So what Jesus is saying here is, "What God puts together, don't divorce."

a) The passage misused

I've heard this verse misused so many times by people. I've even seen it misused in books. They say, "God didn't put our marriage together in the first place, so we can get a divorce." I wish I could tell you how many times I've heard people say that! That kind of logic totally violates the whole intent of the passage. This isn't talking about how you view each other, this is God laying down the truth about marriage and saying, "I make marriages, so you better not take them apart!" And He isn't necessarily talking about Christian marriages or non-Christian marriages. He's saying, "I make all marriages. I'm the One who puts two people together into a union."

You see, marriage is a God-ordained institution. I believe that every marriage—whether it's a Christian marriage or a pagan marriage—is an act of God. It is God who makes a

13

man and a woman so complement each other that they have the capacity to enjoy each other, to be fulfilled by each other, to be the strength for each other's weaknesses, and to produce children to procreate the world. I believe it is a miracle of God that every union exists. Every time a couple comes together and experiences the joy of companionship, friendship, sex, or whatever else, they are experiencing the miracle of God—the miracle that a man should so love a woman and a woman so love a man, that they can abandon themselves to each other in the fullness of a meaningful relationship. Even unbelieving people can enjoy the joy, the thrill, and the meaningfulness of a loving union.

So every marriage is a miracle of God. There is no issue about whether or not you got married "in the will of God." That isn't what Jesus is saying here in verse 6. He is simply defining that in the very beginning God said, "I make marriages." And even when pagans get a divorce, they are ripping apart something that God put together just as much as if Christians were doing it.

b) The point compared

The fact that God makes every marriage can be compared to the birth of a child. I believe that every child born into the world is a creature of God. God created everyone, right? It doesn't matter if the parents are both unbelievers, or even if they're pagans in some tribe in the middle of Africa. Their child is still a miracle of God. The same thing is true of marriage. The marriage that produces the child is an act of God whereby two complementary people are brought together to enjoy the fullness of human life. Marriage is just as much an act of God as birth. In fact, I believe that abortion is to childbirth what divorce is to marriage. As abortion kills the creation of God, so does divorce. And this is exactly what Jesus is saying in verse 6b, "What, therefore, God hath joined together, let not man put asunder." In other words, "You better not break up a marriage—yours or anybody else's—because you're tampering with the work of Almighty God."

So the Pharisees came to Jesus and asked, "Is it lawful for a man to put away [or 'divorce'] his wife for every cause?" (Matt. 19:3b). Jesus answered them by saying, "Listen to what God said. He said, 'Marriage is one man for one woman, it is a strong bond, it is one flesh, and I am the One that makes marriages. So if you tear them apart, you're destroying what I made and placing yourself into a very, very serious position.' "

If you ever decide to go out and fool around with somebody else's husband or wife, just remember this: If you break up a marriage, you break up something created by God. And don't come up with any nonsense about the Lord's leading you. I just hate it when I hear people say, ''The Lord led us out of our marriages and brought us together.'' The Lord doesn't do that. They are in direct violation of what the Lord created.

What Jesus is doing, then, is taking the Pharisees all the way back to the beginning to see what God had to say on the subject of divorce. And instead of losing credibility with the people, as the Pharisees had hoped, He gains it, doesn't He? He simply reiterates what God said in Genesis and makes the Pharisees look stupid by saying, ''Haven't you read this?''

I say the same thing to you: Before you ever think about divorce, or if you're even now trying to decide whether divorce is right or wrong—have you read this? I think the Word of God is very clear on this issue.

Focusing on the Facts

1. What are the three basic reasons why marriages were held together more in the past than they are today? What has happened to change each of these forces (see pp. 2–3)?

2. As Christians, we have basically two choices regarding the issue of divorce. One option is to give in to the world's system. What is the other option (see p. 4)?

3. What are the reasons some Christians either raise or lower the biblical standard for divorce (see p. 4)?

4. What is significant in Matthew 19:1–2 as it relates to Jesus' Galilean ministry (see p. 5)?

5. What do the ''sayings'' of 19:1 refer to? What are the other great discourses in Matthew that are ended in a way similar to 19:1a (see p. 5)?

6. What is the name of the river that splits the land of Palestine down the middle? What two large bodies of water is it connected to (see p. 6)?

7. Where was Jesus going when He left Galilee? What route was He going to take? What was the name of the region He was entering into (see p. 6)?

8. What did the Jews call Perea? Why (see p. 6)?

9. Why would the Jews traveling from Galilee to Judea first go out of their way to the east instead of traveling directly south (see p. 7)?

10. As Jesus began His Perean ministry, why would there have been many Jews traveling this same route to Jerusalem (see p. 7)?

11. What was the purpose of Jesus' healings referred to in Matthew 19:2 (see p. 7)?

12. Why did the Pharisees hate Jesus so much (see p.7)?

13. What two objectives do the Pharisees have in mind when they question Him in Matthew 19:3? How do they plan to carry out these objectives (see pp. 7–10)?

14. Did every rabbi have the same view of divorce? Which rabbi had the most popular view among the people? What was his view of divorce (see p. 8)?

15

15. How did Jesus' view of divorce compare to the Pharisees' view (see pp. 8–9)?

16. How did the Pharisees hope to discredit Jesus (see p. 9)?

17. Why was Jesus such a problem to the Pharisees (see p. 9)?

18. In the Pharisees' plot to destroy Jesus, what is significant about the region He is in and the particular question they ask Him in Matthew 19:3 (see pp. 9–10)?

19. Instead of immediately answering the Pharisees' question from His own authority, Jesus quoted another source. What source did He quote (see p. 10)?

20. In what way was Jesus sarcastic in answering the Pharisees' attack (see p. 11)?

21. What verses does Jesus use in reaffirming God's law against divorce (see p. 11)?

22. What four reasons does Jesus give to show why it is not lawful to divorce for any cause (see pp. 11–14)?

23. What was God's intention in creating only one man and one woman— without any spares (see p. 11)?

24. Why was divorce for Adam and Eve inadvisable (see p. 11)?

25. What two basic ideas are inherent in the Hebrew word for "cleave" (see p. 12)?

26. What is the literal meaning of the Hebrew word *kiddushin*? Why do the Jews use this word to refer to marriage (see p. 12)?

27. What is the significance of the fact that in marriage two people become one flesh? How is this oneness best visualized (see p. 13)?

28. If two people become one person in marriage, what does divorce produce (see p. 13)?

29. The Greek word *chōrizō* is translated "put asunder" in the KJV.* What is a better translation of this word (see p. 13)?

30. What is wrong with the logic of someone who tries to justify a divorce by saying, "God didn't put my marriage together in the first place, so I can get a divorce" (see p. 13)?

31. When non-Christians get divorced, are they tearing apart something created by God? Explain (see pp. 13–14).

32. Complete the following: _____ is to childbirth what _____ is to marriage (see p. 14).

33. What would you say to a couple who claimed that the Lord was leading them to get a divorce (see pp. 14–15)?

Pondering the Principles

1. Take a moment right now to evaluate your home environment by writing down as many words as you can think of that describe both the positive

*King James Version.

and negative characteristics. Did you write down more positive or more negative characteristics? In prayer, thank God for the positive characteristics and ask Him to strengthen and enable you to work on those characteristics in your home which aren't pleasing to Him. Wives, what can you do to make the home a place that your husband and children enjoy? Husband, what can you do to make your wife and children happy to have you home? Commit yourself to create an atmosphere in your home that meets the spiritual, emotional, and physical needs of all its members.

2. If you were to jump out of an airplane without a parachute, what would happen to you? Why? When you violate a law of nature you will suffer consequences, won't you? The same thing is true of God's laws. Christians who violate God's laws against divorce will suffer consequences, won't they? Now, God forgives our sins (1 John 1:9), but our actions still produce consequences. What are some examples of the consequences of divorce?

3. When the Pharisees questioned Jesus about His view of divorce, Jesus quoted what God had said from the beginning of mankind. God's standard hadn't changed from Adam to Christ, and it hasn't changed from Christ to our present day. So that you will be better prepared to handle the world's pressure to conform you to its standards of divorce, memorize and meditate on what Jesus says in Matthew 19:4–6: "Have ye not read that he who made them at the beginning, made them male and female; and said, For this cause shall a man leave father and mother, and shall cleave to his wife, and they two shall be one flesh? Wherefore, they are no more two, but one flesh. What, therefore, God hath joined together, let not man put asunder."

2
Jesus' Teaching on Divorce— Part 2

Outline

Introduction
A. The Objective of the Pastor
B. The Obligation of the Parishioners

Review
I. The Attack
   A. The Pharisees' Attempt to Discredit Jesus
   B. The Pharisees' Attempt to Destroy Jesus
II. The Answer
   A. God's Law Against Divorce Reiterated
      1. One man for one woman
      2. A strong bond
      3. One flesh
      4. A work of God

Lesson
B. God's Law Against Divorce Reaffirmed
      1. The commandments of Exodus 20
         a) The act
            (1) The commandment against adultery
            (2) The consequence of adultery
         b) The attitude
      2. The curse of Genesis 3:16
         a) Marriage before the Fall
            (1) Headship/submission
            (2) Co-regency
         b) Marriage at the Fall
            (1) The woman as leader
            (2) The man as follower
         c) Marriage after the Fall
            (1) The confusion about the curse
            (2) The content of the curse
               (*a*) Man's despotic rule
                  i) Defined
                  ii) Discussed
                  iii) Demonstrated
               (*b*) Woman's desire to control
                  i) The word explained
                  ii) The word examined

3. The condemnation of Malachi 2
   a) The subject of God's indictment
   b) The object of God's hate
4. The characterization of Hosea
   a) Hosea's family
   b) Hosea's ambivalence
      (1) Anger
      (2) Love
      (3) Anger
      (4) Love
   c) Hosea's covenant
5. The commitment of Ephesians 5
   a) The duty of the wife
   b) The duty of the husband

Introduction

A. The Objective of the Pastor

Young men and pastors alike very often ask me the question, "What do you feel is your primary role as a pastor? What is it that you're trying to accomplish with your people?" Well, I believe that my primary objective with the congregation is to bring the people to a point in their conscious mind where they are generally submissive to the Word of God. I want to get them to believe that the Bible is the infallible, authoritative, inerrant, holy Word of God—so that when the Bible speaks, the argument is over. People must see that the Bible speaks authoritatively and that they are to respond to it and obey it. If I, as a pastor, can just get people to make a general commitment to the authority of the Word of God, then I can introduce any principle out of the Word of God, and they are bound by that heart commitment to abide by it.

Now that's important to articulate, because when we come to the subject of divorce, we must remember that God is speaking just as authoritatively as He ever spoke in any other time. That fact has been somewhat undermined, because we have been hearing so many different views about this subject.

B. The Obligation of the Parishioners

An unholy church membership tends to want more and more concessions. In many churches, they conveniently eliminate the Bible, reinterpret it, or say, "Well, that part on divorce was a cultural issue. We can't hold to that anymore. It isn't that serious."

To begin with, I want to affirm to you where we stand at Grace Church: When God speaks, we listen! There's really no debate about that. We are called to submit to the authority of the Word of God. So when the Word of God speaks, we willingly, anxiously, lovingly, eagerly, happily, and joyfully submit—knowing that in obedience there is great blessedness.

19

As we open the pages of our Bibles to Matthew 19, we're reminded of what God teaches about divorce. Our response is to be one of submission to God's Word. Jesus said, "Man shall not live by bread alone, but by every word that proceedeth out of the mouth of God" (Matt. 4:4*b*). We're to live by *every* word that comes out of God's mouth, including the essential words He has given us on the subject of divorce. The fact that divorce is an epidemic, that it is all around us, that we are all touched by it, and that we are all threatened by its devastating impact does not change God's Word one bit. And the sooner God's people begin to obey His Word, the sooner they're going to experience the fullness of His blessing.

God's Word is just as true on the subject of divorce as it is on the subject of salvation or anything else. People eagerly run under the truth of redemption and forgiveness, but want to run out from under the truth about divorce and holy living. However, we cannot so dichotomize the revelation of God.

Review

In our last lesson we noted that in Matthew 19 the Lord begins a new dimension in His ministry. For several years He has been ministering in Galilee, but now He starts on His journey to Jerusalem—to His death and resurrection. To make this journey, He crosses over the Jordan River and moves south into "Judea beyond the Jordan," or the area of Perea (lit., "the beyond"). Chapters 19 and 20 tell us about His Perean ministry. And it is there that He is confronted in 19:3 by those who were forever on the aggressive to discredit and destroy Him—His archenemies, the Pharisees.

I. THE ATTACK (v. 3; see pp. 7–10)

In our last lesson we saw that the Pharisees didn't come to Jesus asking an honest question. They came to test Him. They weren't truth seekers looking for answers. They had two things in mind when they asked the question, "Is it lawful for a man to put away his wife for every cause?"

A. The Pharisees' Attempt to Discredit Jesus (see pp. 8–9)

The popular view among the people was that you could shed your wife for any reason. The Pharisees, knowing Jesus' views on divorce, asked their question in hopes that Jesus would become instantly unpopular and be discredited as holding too narrow a line.

But not only were the Pharisees seeking to discredit Jesus, they had another part to their plan.

B. The Pharisees' Attempt to Destroy Jesus (see pp. 9–10)

Perea was a territory ruled by Herod Antipas, who was illegitimately married to a woman who was not only his brother's wife, but also a blood relative. So Herod's marriage was adultery, wife stealing, and incest. When John the Baptist confronted this union he was imprisoned. Eventually he had his head chopped off. The

20

Pharisees, then, were hoping that they could get Jesus to take a strong stand against divorce and perhaps even lose His head too.

So the Pharisees came with the idea of testing Jesus—hoping He'd fail the test, lose His popularity, and even lose His head. But Jesus didn't evade the issue; He answered them.

II. THE ANSWER (vv. 4-6; see pp. 10-15)

The Pharisees asked Jesus a question, so He gave them a direct answer—but His omniscient mind grasped an answer that made Him come out ahead and not them. Instead of putting Himself on the line, He went back to Genesis, recited the standard laid down by the eternal God, and made it very difficult for the people to take issue with Him. Jesus let God speak, so that in the eyes of the people His answer was not His own opinion; it was the revelation of God.

A. God's Law Against Divorce Reiterated (see pp. 10-15)

In answering the Pharisees, Jesus quoted out of Genesis and gave four reasons why it is not lawful to divorce.

1. One man for one woman (v. 4; see pp. 11-12)

"Have ye not read that he who made them at the beginning, made them male and female?" The first reason not to divorce is that when God created the ideal situation, He created one male and one female—no spares! There weren't any alternatives or options. That's the way God designed it.

2. A strong bond (v. 5a; see p. 12)

"For this cause shall a man leave father and mother, and shall cleave to his wife." The word "cleave" means "to glue something together." God intended two people to be glued together.

3. One flesh (vv. 5b-6a; see p. 13)

"They two shall be one flesh? Wherefore, they are no more two, but one flesh." In marriage, two people become one person—and one can't be divided.

4. A work of God (v. 6b; see pp. 13-14)

"What, therefore, God hath joined together, let not man put asunder [or 'divorce']." Marriage is a work of God!

So, when confronted with the question, "Is it lawful for a man to put away [divorce] his wife for any cause?" Jesus said, "Don't you know that God said, 'One man-one woman, strong bond, one flesh, and marriage is My divine work'? So don't divorce!"

Verse 6 ends Jesus' answer to the question of the Pharisees in verse 3. But before we go on to verse 7, I want to show you how God consistently reaffirms His law against divorce throughout the Old Testament.

Lesson

B. God's Law Against Divorce Reaffirmed

When God laid down the idea of one man-one woman for life, strong bond, one flesh, work of God, no divorce—He really affirmed it. Let me show you how.

1. The commandments of Exodus 20

   a) The Act

   (1) The commandment against adultery

   In Exodus 20:14 God says, "Thou shalt not commit adultery." Adultery has to do with a sexual relationship outside of a marriage union by married people. So when a married person has a relationship with someone other than his partner, that is adultery. And God said, "Thou shalt not commit adultery." In other words, never violate marriage. That is one of the most important laws God ever established.

   (2) The consequence of adultery

   Leviticus 20:10*b* gives us the consequence of adultery in the Old Testament, "the adulterer and the adulteress shall surely be put to death." The only sin that could break a marriage, then, was adultery. Why? Because according to God's law it resulted in death. And there is little question that death ended a marriage.

   So God says, "One man-one woman, strong bond, one flesh, work of God, no divorce. And if you commit adultery, you'll lose your life!" You see, there really was no provision for divorce. In the case of adultery, however, execution would free the innocent partner to marry again. The point is this: All sexual sin is serious, but the violation of a marriage is fatal. That gives us God's view of the sanctity of marriage. And He really means what He says.

   b) The attitude

   Taking it a step further, the tenth commandment contains this statement: "Thou shalt not covet thy neighbor's wife" (Ex. 20:17*b*). So God is saying, "Not only are you not to commit adultery, you are not even to *want* to commit adultery. Not only are you not to do it, you're not even to think about it." Jesus reinforces this in Matthew 5:28 when He says, "Whosoever looketh on a woman to lust after her hath committed adultery with her already in his heart."

   Marriage is so sacred, so sacrosanct, so much a separation of two people unto each other, so much a work of God, that any violation of it, in body or in mind, is to violate the command of God. And the priority law of God was that when a person violated marriage in body, he was to be executed on the spot.

22

That's how sacred marriage is. That's the way God designed it from the very beginning. That's His ideal—His perfect plan.

It seems awfully hard for people to live up to God's ideal for marriage, doesn't it? Marriage seems to be nothing but a battleground—a place where war rages all the time. People seem to always be on the verge of splitting up—whether they're in the church or not. In fact, it's a fairly common problem among those who call themselves Christians. Why? Well, let me take you back to Genesis and show you why we have such a difficult time maintaining God's ideal.

2. The curse of Genesis 3:16

   a) Marriage before the Fall

      (1) Headship/submission

         After God created man and woman, Genesis 1:28a tells us, "And God blessed them, and God said unto them, Be fruitful, and multiply, and fill the earth, and subdue it; and have dominion." When God made man and woman, He made them as a perfect complement.

         Man was created first (Gen. 2:7), and the woman was made to be his helper (Gen. 2:18), his support. Man was to be the strong one, the provider, the leader, the protector. This is affirmed for us in 1 Corinthians 11:3–9 where the Word of God very clearly lays out the fact that "Christ is the head of every man, and the man is the head of a woman, and God is the head of Christ" (v. 3, NASB). It is also affirmed for us in 1 Timothy 2:11–14 where it says that the man is the head of the woman by virtue of the creation of God. That's the way it was in the very beginning.

      (2) Co-regency

         If you look again at Genesis 1:28, you really don't see man's headship and woman's submission: "And God blessed them, and God said unto them, Be fruitful, and multiply, and fill the earth, and subdue it; and have dominion." In other words, there was a co-regency. There was such an incredibly perfect harmony, such a bliss of union between man and woman, that there was no conflict or friction. Man was fully man in every dimension. He was the strong one, the protector, the provider. And woman was all that God created her to be as man's source of strength and help. Their relationship was in such perfect, God-created harmony that it could be said they ruled together.

There was a majesty about that relationship. The headship of the man and the submission of the woman was so blended into oneness that it could be said they multiplied *together*,

23

subdued the earth *together,* and ruled the earth *together.*
There wasn't any discord at all.

b) Marriage at the Fall

   (1) The woman as leader

In Genesis 3, sin came into the picture, and the perfect relationship in marriage was lost. The woman sinned and took over the leadership. When she was being beguiled by the serpent, she didn't go back to the man and say, "Adam, I need your protection, your strength, your headship." Instead, she acted independently of him. When she heard Satan tell her that she could know good and evil and be like God, she usurped his place of leadership.

   (2) The man as follower

Once the woman took the place of leadership, the man fell to the place of the follower and followed her in sin. And according to 1 Timothy 2:14*a,* "Adam was not deceived."

So at the Fall there was a reversal of the God-ordained roles. The woman took the lead, the man followed, and sin entered the world. Sin came not only because of an actual act of disobedience toward God but also because of a reversal of the God-ordained roles for the man and the woman.

c) Marriage after the Fall

God cursed the man and the woman because of their sin. The woman was cursed in her childbearing in 3:16*a,* so that she would suffer great pain in bringing forth children. Man was cursed in his breadwinning in 3:17–19, so that he would suffer great pain in bringing forth resources out of the earth. And at the end of 3:16, God pronounces a curse upon the relationship of marriage: "And thy desire shall be to thy husband, and he shall rule over thee."

   (1) The confusion about the curse

People have been confused about what Genesis 3:16*b* means. Most commentators say that the phrase "thy desire" simply refers to "the normal, strong, sexual, psychological desire, attraction, and need that a woman has for her husband." They also say that the phrase "he shall rule over thee" is a normal function of headship where the husband leads his wife. Well, if all of this is just normal and routine, what does it have to do with being cursed? Furthermore, this is not what happens in marriages. A woman does not wonderfully continue to desire her husband with a strong physical attraction while he takes care of all her needs in ruling, supplying, and

24

providing. It just isn't that way. And even if it were, it wouldn't be a curse!

So to find out what God is saying in Genesis 3:16*b*, we have to look a little closer at the text.

(2) The content of the curse

    (*a*) Man's despotic rule

        "And he shall rule over thee."

        i) Defined

            The word "rule" in the Hebrew is *masal*. In the Septuagint (the Greek translation of the Old Testament) the word used is *kathistēmi*, which means "to install in an office" or "to elevate to an official position."

        ii) Discussed

            Since the Fall, man has been installed in an official position as a ruler. Before the Fall, there was a co-regency—a wonderful, blending harmony. So this part of the curse says, "Woman, you stepped out from under your husband. You acted independently. So from now on, the husband is installed as the ruler in your relationship and you're going to have to suffer under his headship." That's the essence of this aspect of the curse. Instead of the wonderful, harmonious ruling that they had known before as co-regents together, man's authority would become perverse and despotic.

        iii) Demonstrated

            You ask, "Is this why there are male chauvinists?" Yes—and there are millions of them. I don't argue with people from the women's liberation movement who try to convince me of the *fact* of male chauvinism—it is worldwide and history long. Since the Fall, men have been installed in a despotic place and have tried to keep women down. All societies of the world (with few exceptions) throughout the history of the world have been male-dominated societies. And in many, many cases, it is an abusive kind of domination. I don't deny it for a moment. It's all part of the curse—men pushing women around.

            Even in the time of our Lord Jesus Christ, women were looked upon, in some cases, as less than animals. And throughout the societies of our contemporary modern world, it is still difficult for women to get any kind of understanding.

Why? Because men continually want to push them down in an unbalanced and improper way. But that's part of the curse!

Marriage was cursed when the roles were reversed in Adam and Eve's sin. Eve took the lead and Adam followed. So God said to the woman, "Because you came out from under the man's leadership, I'm going to curse you by installing him in an office over you. And now that man is sinful, he will tend to carry out that office in a rather brutal way."

(b) Woman's desire to control

"And thy desire shall be to thy husband."

i) The word explained

The "desire" here isn't normal, sexual desire. In fact the husband usually has a stronger sexual desire than the wife. It's not talking about sexual desire. The Arabic root for the word translated "desire" means "to seek control." So the curse is this: The man is installed as the ruler, but the woman is going to seek to control him.

Once Adam and Eve sinned and God pronounced the curse, the battle of the sexes has been raging on. There is conflict in marriage because the woman is still trying to get out from under man's authority and rule him, and man is trying to keep her down where she is. So we not only have male chauvinism, but we also have women's rebellions. They run through all of history.

ii) The word examined

A good way to understand the usage of the word "desire" is to look at Genesis 4:7b where the identical word, in the same grammatical construction, appears. Cain is being warned by the Lord, and He says, "Sin lieth at the door. And unto thee shall be his [sin personified] desire, and thou shalt rule over him [sin]." This is the only time other than Genesis 3:16 where this particular word for "desire" is used in the Pentateuch. What it's saying is, "Cain, sin desires to control you, but you must rule it." It's the same idea as in 3:16 where the woman desires to control the man, but he must rule her.

So the marriage of Adam and Eve was cursed at the moment of their sin, when they reversed their God-ordained roles. Since that time there has been conflict and tension in marriage as the

26

woman seeks supremacy and the man seeks suppression. That's why we have divorce—because conflict became inevitable.

3. The condemnation of Malachi 2

Moving from the beginning of the Old Testament in Genesis, let's go to the end of the Old Testament to the book of Malachi and see if God feels any differently about marriage.

a) The subject of God's indictment (v. 14)

In Malachi 2, God is indicting the people of Israel because they were being unfaithful to their wives. In verse 14 God says through the prophet Malachi, "The LORD hath been witness between thee and the wife of thy youth, against whom thou hast dealt treacherously; yet is she thy companion, and the wife of thy covenant." Notice the first part of the verse, "The Lord hath been witness between thee and the wife of thy youth." That's just what our Lord said in Matthew 19:6 when He said that marriage is God's putting people together. The Lord is the witness to a marriage, confirming the covenant. And Israel was dealing treacherously with the wives of their covenant—their companions.

b) The object of God's hate (v. 16)

In verse 16, God's view is recited: "For the Lord, the God of Israel, saith that he hateth putting away [or 'divorce']." We would expect that, wouldn't we? In Genesis we learn that God saw marriage as one man-one woman, a strong bond, one flesh, a work of God, no divorce. Just because the curse came and marriage was cursed, that doesn't mean God changed His mind. Even though the battle is on, God's standard hasn't changed. He hates divorce.

Verse 16 continues, "For one covereth violence with his garment." In the Hebrew, this phrase is literally saying that when you get into a divorce, you splatter your clothes with violence. The picture is that of a life-and-death hand-to-hand struggle in which your garments would be splattered with blood. In other words, when you divorce, you splatter your garments with sin. Why? Because God hates divorce. But that is to be expected, because over in 3:6*a* He says, "For I am the Lord, I change not."

You say, "Well, what do I do if the conflict in my marriage gets too great to handle? What if I'm constantly being defrauded?" God's Word deals with that situation, too.

4. The characterization of Hosea

a) Hosea's family

The Lord speaks to Hosea in 1:2 and says, "Go, take a wife. However, she's going to turn out to be a harlot, and you're going to wind up with a couple of illegitimate children." Verses 3–4 tell us that Hosea went and took Gomer, the daughter of Diblaim, and they had a son named Jezreel. God told Hosea to name their son Jezreel because He was going to bring vengeance on Israel for their harlotries.

Hosea was to be a living illustration of the relationship between God and Israel. Hosea married a woman who turned out to be a prostitute and gave him illegitimate children. In a similar way, God married Israel, who turned out to be a harlot involved in all kinds of illegitimate affairs and relationships, producing all kinds of illegitimate results. So Hosea and Gomer became a living parable of God and Israel.

Well, they were married and they had a son by the name of Jezreel. Then according to verses 6–9, Gomer had two more children, "And she conceived again, and bore a daughter. And God said unto him, Call her name Lo-ruhamah [which means 'no mercy']. . . . Now when she had weaned Lo-ruhamah, she conceived and bore a son. Then said God, Call his name Lo-ammi [which means 'not mine' or 'not my people']" (vv. 6*a*, 8–9*a*). How's that for two kids? No Mercy and Not Mine. Hosea was saying, "I'll show no mercy to that kid, and the other one doesn't belong to me." Illegitimate—both of them.

b) Hosea's ambivalence

When Gomer brought home these two illegitimate kids, how do you think he reacted? Well, he loved her and was devoted to her because of his covenant to her in marriage. He was an honorable man, and he wanted to make the most out of his union—even though he was married to a prostitute who gave him two illegitimate children with names that pointed out to the whole world that they were not his.

Hosea's reaction was one of ambivalence, as seen in the following passages.

(1) Anger (2:2–5)

If Hosea is going to react like anybody else, he's going to get mad. There is going to be anger in his heart. And that's exactly what happens in 2:2–5: "Contend with your mother, contend; for she is not my wife, neither am I her husband." In other words, in his anger Hosea says, "I'm not taking any of this. I'm getting out of this deal." Verse 2 continues, "Let her, therefore, put away her harlotry out of her sight, and her adulteries from between her breasts, lest I strip her naked, and set her as in the day that she was born, and make her like a wilderness, and set her like a dry land, and slay her with thirst." In fury he basically says, "Wait till you see what I do to that woman!" His anger was a very normal reaction.

28

Continuing on in verses 4 and 5, Hosea says, "And I will not have mercy upon her children; for they are the children of harlotry. For their mother hath played the harlot. She that conceived them hath done shamefully; for she said, I will go after my lovers, that give me my bread and my water, my wool and my flax, mine oil and my drink." She was in it for one reason—money! She was a prostitute, a streetwalker, a paid harlot.

From Hosea's perspective, it was all over for Gomer. She had devastated this prophet of God by bringing two illegitimate children into his home—two children who would have to bear the stigma of illegitimacy by their very names and the stigma of their mother's reputation. So Hosea is mad—mad at having a prostitute for a wife.

(2) Love (2:6–8)

In verse 6, Hosea shifts gears; "Therefore, behold, I will hedge up thy way with thorns, and make a wall, that she shall not find her paths." In other words, he gets over his anger and desires to keep her from doing it anymore. He gets sort of righteous and decides to become her protector by putting a hedge or wall around her. Then verse 7 says, "And she shall follow after her lovers, but she shall not overtake them; and she shall seek them, but she shall not find them." He's going to make it really hard for her to connect up with her customers.

I've seen situations like this where a man, when he finds out his wife is being unfaithful, tries to close off all her alternatives by getting phone numbers of the men she's sleeping with, calling them up and threatening them, camping out on their doorstep, and writing them letters. I've even known husbands to write letters to the man's employer, saying, "You have a guy in your business who is having a relationship with my wife, breaking up my home, and so on. Is this the kind of place you operate?" In other words they do whatever it takes to close off all the options. And when they come and ask me if they should do those things, I say, "Sure! Why not? Do whatever it takes to get her back."

Hosea tried to do whatever he could to get Gomer back. At the end of verse 7 he says, "Then shall she say, I will go and return to my first husband; for then was it better with me than now." His thinking was this: "If she can't make any contacts out there, she won't be able to make a living. Then she'll want to come back to me because it will be the only option available to her." Now someone might say, "I wouldn't want her on those terms!" Not

Hosea. He wanted her on any terms. Quite a forgiving guy, isn't he?

Verse 8 goes even deeper into Hosea's heart: "For she did not know that I gave her grain, and wine, and oil, and multiplied her silver and gold, which they prepared for Baal." In other words, she didn't know it, but Hosea made sure that Gomer's needs were met by having clothes to wear, food to eat, and money to live on. He took care of her.

Hosea really loved her, didn't he? She's out walking the streets having affairs day and night while he's making sure she has enough to eat, a place to stay, and money to live on. Now I don't know what method he used to do this, but he apparently supplied her needs without her knowing the source.

(3) Anger (2:9-13)

You say, "This guy is too much!" Well, look at verses 9–11a: "Therefore will I return, and take away my grain in its time, and my wine in its season, and will recover my wool and my flax given to cover her nakedness. And now will I uncover her lewdness in the sight of her lovers, and none shall deliver her out of mine hand. I will cause all her mirth to cease." The more he thinks about what he's been paying to support her the angrier he gets. Reverting back to where he started, he says, "I've been giving all of these things to her—Well, no more! I'm going to take away her party and end it all!"

Then in verses 11b–13 a transition is made from Gomer to Israel. In fact, very often in Hosea it's hard to tell whether it's talking about Gomer or Israel, because Hosea's relationship with Gomer is simply a living illustration of God and His relationship to His people Israel.

(4) Love (2:14)

Hosea shifts gears again in verse 14, "Therefore, behold, I will allure her, and bring her into the wilderness, and speak tenderly unto her." This is God with Israel just as much as it is Hosea with Gomer.

Do you know what Hosea is saying he's going to do? He's going to go back and try to court her again. He's going to go find that wretched prostitute and court her—taking her flowers, whispering sweet nothings in her ear, and treating her as if she were a virgin. Incredible!

c) Hosea's covenant

Gomer finally ends up stark naked on a slave block being auctioned off as a prostitute for sale. Hosea shows up in 3:2 and says, "So I bought her for myself for fifteen pieces of

30

silver, and for an homer of barley, and an half homer of barley.'' She went to the highest bidder. Frankly, I think he got a lousy deal, humanly speaking, don't you?

Then verse 3 says, "And I said unto her, Thou shalt abide for me many days.'' Notice that he doesn't say, "Now look, baby, I've got a lot invested in you. One more false move and that's it!'' That's not his approach. Rather, his approach is unconditional. "I covenant that you will be with me for many days.'' Verse 3 continues, "Thou shalt not play the harlot, and thou shalt not be for another man; so will I also be for thee.'' In other words, "You may have fouled up, but I'm still for you because you can't kill that covenant in me.''

I believe that most of us have difficulty with Hosea's forgiving heart because we don't really understand the forgiving heart of God. It's a little like the parable in Matthew 18:23–35 where the man was willing to be forgiven a ten-thousand-talent debt (about ten million dollars) but couldn't forgive his friend of the one-hundred-denarii debt (about eighteen dollars) he owed him. We take it all from God, but we have such a difficult time forgiving others.

So Hosea bought Gomer back, took her as if she were a virgin, and made an unconditional covenant with her. Doesn't that just reinforce the fact that God's standard of no divorce hasn't changed? Up to this point in our study, there is only one sin that could break a marriage—adultery. Why? Because adultery brought death upon the offender.

5. The commitment of Ephesians 5

Ephesians 5:22–33 is a wonderful, pure, blissful text on the subject of marriage. In fact, the standard it sets seems almost impossible with what we know about marriage.

a) The duty of the wife

This section starts out with verse 22: "Wives, submit your-selves unto your own husbands, as unto the Lord.'' That's not easy is it? You say, "I can submit to the guy now and then but 'as unto the Lord'? That's hard! I know the guy, and there are a lot of things about the Lord that are just not true about him. I know he's a Christian, but I have to submit to him 'as unto the Lord'?'' It almost seems far beyond any conception of reality. However, it's simply a reaffirmation of the original creation principle.

Adam, in his perfection, was the vice-regent of God on earth. So verse 22 wonderfully reaffirms the original intention that a wife would be gently, lovingly, meekly, yet strongly submissive to her own husband—recognizing his headship (v. 23) and being subject in everything (v. 24). It takes the woman back to her wonderful role as a submissive helper with the man as a leading head. Together they co-reign on the earth—where neither is diminished, but both are exalted.

b) The duty of the husband

In verse 25 it says, "Husbands, love your wives." Now in the curse, the woman seeks to control and the man seeks to dominate. But here in Ephesians 5, the women want to submit, and the men, rather than seeking to rule, want to love, purify, nourish, and cherish their wives (vv. 25–29). The man is to be the protector, provider, nourisher, lover, and supporter.

The point of this text is that it is a return to the Genesis 1 and 2 design of marriage. You say, "Is it possible?" Yes! It has to be. And the key is Ephesians 5:18 where Paul says, "And be not drunk with wine, in which is excess, but be filled with the Spirit." I believe that when Christ comes into a marriage where two people love Him, and if those two people are controlled by the Holy Spirit, they will fulfill verse 21, "Submitting yourselves one to another in the fear of God."

So we are to keep our marriages together because God says it's a priority—and we want to submit to the authority of the Word of God. As we walk in the Spirit, we will be able to wonderfully submit to one another out of reverence for God. Wives, in the power of the Spirit, can return to the pre-Fall bliss of being wonderfully submissive to their husbands. And husbands can return to the pre-Fall bliss of being loving, caring, nourishing, and cherishing toward their wives. And when sin enters into the relationship, there will be forgiveness as God forgave Israel and as Christ forgives His church.

How to make your marriage what it ought to be

There are two key words to remember to make your marriage what it ought to be.

1. Self-denial

If you go into a marriage demanding your rights, defending yourself, justifying yourself, getting what you want, seeking your own fulfillment, following your own desires, and acquiescing to the temptations of the flesh, you will devastate your union. But when you deny yourself and say no to self, you will be on the right road.

2. Unselfishness

Unselfishness in marriage is being able to say, "I think more of you than I do of me." It's when I'm able to say no to me and yes to my wife. I don't have to justify myself—even if I'm falsely accused. I'm not vengeful, vindictive, or defensive. I'm able to say no to myself and to those things that will drag me

32

away from the covenant that I have made with my wife. I'm able to say no to those things that will lure me away from the love bonds we share. Unselfishness enables me to say no to those things and yes to my wife. Now it doesn't mean that I acquiesce to my partner's stupidity or sin, but I'm to give myself to her needs, her welfare, her best interest.

And remember, when sin arises in a heart of self-denial and unselfishness, it can be resolved—just as it was in Hosea's heart.

Let me close with a verse that should reflect our attitude toward all of Scripture—even when it relates to divorce. It is Isaiah 45:9a, which says, "Woe unto him that striveth [or 'argues'] with his Maker!" It's pretty stupid to argue with God, isn't it? When God says something, whatever it's about, you had better do it, right? Whatever God says about marriage or divorce, do it! Or woe unto you if you argue with Him. By the way, the word "woe" means "damn" or "curse." So the person who argues with his Maker will be damned or cursed. After all, if God made you, He knows how to make you work best, right? If He's the manufacturer, He has your operating manual.

My job as a pastor and teacher is to bring you under submission to the authority of God's Word. And I've told you what God says about divorce. Now all I can say is, "Woe be unto the person who fights or argues with his Maker!" God seeks your good so you *will* be blessed if you're obedient to His holy Word.

Focusing on the Facts

1. What is one of the primary objectives a pastor must have with his congregation? Why (see p. 19)?

2. As Christians, what is our obligation to the Word of God (see p. 19)?

3. Is God's Word as trustworthy on the subject of divorce as it is on the subjects of redemption and forgiveness? Why is this so important to realize (see p. 20)?

4. The Pharisees were attempting to d_____ and d_____ Jesus by asking their questions about divorce in Matthew 19:3 (see p. 20).

5. What was Jesus' strategy in answering the Pharisees' question by quoting out of Genesis (see p. 21)?

6. What are the four reasons Jesus gives from Genesis to show why it is not lawful to divorce (see p. 21)?

7. Do any of the Ten Commandments reveal to us how God views marriage? If so, which one(s), and what is revealed (see pp. 22–23)?

8. What is the consequence of adultery in the Old Testament? What verse supports this (see p. 22)?

9. In the Old Testament, what is the only sin that could break a marriage? Why (see p. 22)?

10. What verses teach that God is just as concerned about the act of adultery as He is thoughts of adultery (see p. 22)?

11. Why do people have such a difficult time maintaining God's ideal in marriage (see pp. 23–26)?

12. How would you describe the relationship between man and woman before the Fall (see pp. 23–24)?

13. What New Testament references support the headship of the man and the submission of the woman (see p. 23)?

14. Why wasn't man's headship and woman's submission real obvious in Genesis 1:28 (see p. 23)?

15. In the Fall, how was there a reversal of the God-ordained roles of man and woman (see p. 24)?

16. What were the elements of the curse as it applied specifically to the man and to the woman? What were the two elements of the curse as it related to their relationship with each other (see pp. 24–26)?

17. How do most commentators interpret Genesis 3:16*b*? What are the problems with this interpretation? What is a more likely interpretation (see pp. 24–26)?

18. Based on the elements of the curse, why is there a conflict in marriage (see pp.26–27)?

19. What is the biblical explanation for the existence of male chauvinism and women's rebellions throughout all of history (see p. 26)?

20. What verse in Genesis supports the interpretation of the word "desire" in Genesis 3:16 to mean "to seek control" (see p. 26)?

21. Why was God indicting Israel in Malachi 2:14–16? According to verse 16 what does God hate (see p. 27)?

22. What does the following phrase refer to, "for one covereth violence with his garment" (Mal. 2:16*b*; see p. 27)?

23. What principle of marriage and divorce is illustrated by the life of Hosea (see p. 28)?

24. According to the book of Hosea, is divorce required in the case of adultery? Explain (see pp. 28–31).

25. The relationship between Hosea and Gomer was a living illustration of what important relationship (see p. 28)?

26. What were the names of Hosea's two illegitimate children? What do their names mean (see p. 28)?

27. Describe Hosea's reactions to Gomer in chapter 2 (see pp. 28–30).

28. What lesson can be learned from Hosea's response to Gomer in Hosea 3:2–3 (see pp. 30–31)?

29. Why do most people have such a difficult time understanding Hosea's forgiving heart (see p. 31)?

30. Ephesians 5:22–33 is simply a _____ of the original creation principle (see p. 32).

31. Is it possible for a marriage to be what God originally intended it to be? What is the key (see pp. 32–33)?

32. What two key words must be remembered if you are to make your marriage what it ought to be (see pp. 32–33)?

33. What does Isaiah say about someone who argues with his Maker (see p. 33; Isa. 45:9a)?

Pondering the Principles

1. As a Christian, how are you to respond to God's Word? Why? What are you currently doing to increase your knowledge of God's principles for living? What more could you personally be doing (e.g., meditation, memorization, systematic personal Bible study, daily Bible reading)? Commit yourself to be diligent in what you are already doing in the area of Bible study, and also to begin to do something which will add to your knowledge of God's Word.

2. God's Word gives us answers to many of the issues we face each day. And most of the time, God's perspective is just the opposite of the world's perspective. For example, consider the following issues and compare the world's view with God's view: *obtaining wealth* (Prov. 23:4; 1 Tim. 6:6–11); *buying on credit* (Prov. 22:7b; Rom. 13:8a; 1 Cor. 7:23); *working mothers* (1 Tim. 5:8, 14; Titus 2:4–5); *self-esteem* (Prov. 16:19; 30:32; Isa. 51:1; 57:15; Matt. 23:12; James 4:6, 10; 1 Pet. 5:5–6); *drunkenness* (Prov. 20:1; Isa. 5:11–12, 22; Luke 21:34; Rom. 13:13; 1 Cor. 5:11; 6:9–10; Gal. 5:19–21; Eph. 5:18a); *leisure* (Ps. 90:12; 1 Cor. 15:58; Eph. 5:15–16); *homosexuality* (Lev. 20:13; Rom. 1:26–32; 1 Cor. 6:9–10); *abortion* (Ex. 20:13; cf. Ps. 139:13–16); *sexual activity before marriage* (1 Cor. 6:13, 15, 18; Eph. 5:3; 1 Thess. 4:3; Gal. 5:19–21); *adultery* (Ex. 20:14; Lev. 20:10; Gal. 5:19–21); *divorce* (Mal. 2:16; Matt. 5:31–32; 19:3–12; Luke 16:18). Is your perspective on these issues closer to the world's or to God's? What must you do to avoid the encroachment of the world's views into your thinking (see Ps. 119:9–16)?

3. Briefly review what marriage was like before the Fall. What was the role of the man? the woman? How were these roles reversed at the Fall? According to Genesis 3:16b how did the curse affect both the man and the woman in their marriage relationship? How is a pre-Fall marriage relationship possible today (see Eph. 5:18–33)? Commit yourself to fulfill your God-ordained role in marriage and to be continually controlled by the Spirit of God so that your marriage will become all that God intended it to be.

4. If the conflict in your marriage becomes almost impossible to handle, consider how God wants you to respond to the situation. How did Hosea respond to an unfaithful partner (unfaithful to the point of prostitution)? Look up the following passages on forgiveness: Proverbs 19:11; Matthew 6:14–15; 18:21–35; Mark 11:25; Luke 17:3–4; Ephesians 4:32; Colossians 3:13. If you're having problems in your marriage, thank God for forgiving you of all your sins and then ask Him to help you to forgive any wrongs done to you. Now, make a commitment to continue to forgive your partner as God continues to forgive you!

35

5. The key to a harmonious marriage is found in the following words: self-denial and unselfishness. Memorize and meditate on the following passage to better enable you to cultivate harmony in your home: "Do nothing from selfishness or empty conceit, but with humility of mind let each of you regard one another as more important than himself; do not merely look out for your own personal interests, but also for the interests of others" (Phil. 2:3–4, NASB).

3

Jesus' Teaching on Divorce—
Part 3

Outline

Review
  I. The Attack
 II. The Answer

Lesson
III. The Argument
   A. The Malice of the Pharisees
   B. The Misinterpretation of Deuteronomy 24:1–4
     1. The explicit command against remarriage
       a) Discovered by the proper translation
       b) Disguised by the improper translation
     2. The erroneous cause for divorce
       a) "Uncleanness" interpreted
         (1) By Jewish tradition
         (2) By the context
       b) "Uncleanness" investigated
IV. The Affirmation
   A. The Permission of Moses
     1. The restriction of his permission
     2. The reasons behind his permission
       a) God's grace
       b) Hard-hearted adultery
   B. The Proliferation of Adultery
     1. The principle repeated by Jesus
     2. The principle reaffirmed by Paul

Review

I. THE ATTACK (v. 3; see pp. 7–10)

"The Pharisees also came unto him, testing him, and saying unto him, Is it lawful for a man to put away [or 'divorce'] his wife for every cause?"

II. THE ANSWER (vv. 4–6; see pp. 10–15, 20–33)

"And he answered and said unto them, Have ye not read that he who made them at the beginning, made them male and female; and said, For this cause shall a man leave father and mother, and shall cleave to his wife, and they two shall be one flesh? Wherefore, they are no more two, but one flesh. What, therefore, God hath joined together, let not man put asunder [or 'divorce']."

What makes a marriage?

Jesus said, "What, therefore, God hath joined together, let not man [divorce]." Well, what is it that makes a marriage?

A. The Sex Act

Some people have said that a sexual relationship is what makes a marriage. They say, "Once you have a sex relationship with someone, you're automatically married because 'one flesh' is the essence of marriage." But that's not true.

   1. The recognition of fornication

   If sex made a marriage, there would be no such thing as fornication. Why? Because two unmarried people who have a sexual relationship wouldn't be committing fornication, they'd be getting married. But God says that when two unmarried people commit a sexual act together, it is sin—fornication.

   2. The responsibility of fornication

   In Exodus 22:16—17 it says that if a man lies with a virgin, he is to marry her, because he has taken her virginity. In other words, just lying with her doesn't cause a marriage, because he is to go out and marry her. If her father refuses him, then he is to pay him a sufficient sum to compensate for what he has stolen from his daughter. However, the man is not seen as being married by the sex act. Rather, he is responsible to get married at a later time.

   3. The result of adultery

   Adultery does not dissolve a marriage. In Malachi 2:16 it says that God hates divorce. And in 2:14 it says, "The Lord hath been witness between thee and the wife of thy youth, against whom thou hast dealt treacherously; yet is she thy companion, and the wife of thy covenant." What this is saying is this, "Even though you committed adultery and dealt treacherously against your wife, she is still your wife." Why? "Because she is the wife of your covenant."

So it is not the sex act that makes a marriage. What is it?

B. The Marital Covenant

The coming together of two people who pledge a lifelong covenant of companionship is what makes a marriage. The Bible affirms that! Marriage is a covenantal arrangement for lifelong companionship. So when a person has a sex relationship with someone, that doesn't make a marriage. And when a married person has sex with someone other than his partner, that doesn't make another marriage. It's a sin against the covenant of marriage.

> The binding covenant of a lifelong pledge of companionship constitutes a marriage. And any time two people make that covenant—whether they're saved or not—they come together in a God-ordained, God-created union which should never be divorced.

Lesson

III. THE ARGUMENT (v. 7)

"They say unto him, Why did Moses then command to give a writing of divorcement, and to put her away [or 'to divorce her']?"

A. The Malice of the Pharisees

What amazes me is that the Pharisees are not at all interested in the divine ideal of marriage that the Lord has just presented. The Lord has affirmed lifelong marriage and said in essence that God hates divorce. But the Pharisees aren't interested in the divine ideal, they're only interested in the exception. That's how it is with sinful people. They're not interested in abiding by the law, they're only interested in finding the loopholes.

The Pharisees are classic cases of people looking for loopholes in God's law. On the one hand, they want to be thought of as keeping God's law and being in God's favor. But on the other hand, they try to find every way out they possibly can. So they're only interested in the exception. Why? In order to accommodate their lust and their multiple divorces and adulteries.

Also, notice again how wily the Pharisees are in seeking to pit Jesus against Moses. If they can do that, it will be another way they can discredit Jesus with the people. Why? Because the people's reverence for Moses is second only to God. So, if they can set Jesus against Moses, they will have accomplished something significant.

B. The Misinterpretation of Deuteronomy 24:1–4

When the Pharisees asked the question, "Why did Moses then command to give a writing of divorcement, and to [divorce her]?" (v. 7), they were basically asking, "If all You say is true, then why did Moses command divorce?" Now that's a loaded question, because Moses didn't command divorce! You say, "What are the Pharisees referring to? What did Moses say?" Well, the passage they had in mind was Deuteronomy 24:1–4—the only passage relative to Moses that gives any definitive statement relating to divorce.

1. The explicit command against remarriage

   a) Discovered by the proper translation

   In order to understand this passage we have to depart from the King James Version (which improperly translates these verses) and use the more proper translation of the *New American Standard Bible*.

Beginning in verses 1–2 it says, "When a man takes a wife and marries her, and it happens that she finds no favor in his eyes because he has found some indecency in her, and he writes her a certificate of divorce and puts it in her hand and sends her out from his house, and she leaves his house and goes and becomes another man's wife."

Notice at this point that there has been no editorializing on this incident. The text does not say who was right or wrong. It also does not say that God commanded the man to divorce his wife or that he had to divorce her or that he did the right thing in divorcing her. There is absolutely no editorial comment at all—from God or Moses. The first two verses simply state an illustration of a man who wanted to unload his wife because he found some indecency in her. After he wrote her a divorce certificate and sent her out of the house, she remarried.

Now let's continue the story in verses 3–4, "And if the latter husband turns against her and writes her a certificate of divorce and puts it in her hand and sends her out of his house, or if the latter husband dies who took her to be his wife, *then* her former husband who sent her away is not allowed to take her again to be his wife, since she has been defiled" (emphasis added). This is the first comment on the entire incident. Husband number one is not allowed to remarry his former wife.

So, there *is* a command in Deuteronomy 24. But it's *not* a command to divorce; it's a command not to remarry under specific circumstances. The man in this illustration is not permitted to remarry his former wife. Even if husband number two dies and makes her a widow, she cannot go back to husband number one. Why? The end of verse 4 says, "Since she has been defiled; for that is an abomination before the Lord, and you shall not bring sin on the land which the Lord your God gives you as an inheritance." To remarry that woman would be a sin because she was defiled.

b) Disguised by the improper translation

The Jewish rabbis did not properly translate this passage. They interpreted it as a command to divorce. In other words, when husband number one found an indecency in his wife, he divorced her because he was commanded to do so. Well, it's interesting that the King James translators interpreted this passage the same way. Verse 1 reads, "When a man hath taken a wife, and married her, and it come to pass that she find no favor in his eyes, because he hath found some uncleanness in her; then let him write her a bill of divorcement, and give it in her hand, and send her out of his house." So the King James translators picked up the same traditional rabbinic interpretation—but that is not the way the text reads in the Hebrew.

The protasis/apodosis (condition/conclusion or if/then) is not correctly translated in the King James Version. The rendering of the text has nothing to do with a command to divorce. It says, "*If* a man does this, and *if* he does this, and *if* he does this, *then* he can't take her back." The command is clearly that he can't remarry his former wife, not that he should divorce her!

So the Pharisees misinterpreted Deuteronomy 24:1–4, upon which they based their multitudinous divorces. The passage does not condone divorce, advocate divorce, or command divorce. The passage regulates remarriage!

2. The erroneous cause for divorce

In Deuteronomy 24:1 we find a cause for the divorce. It says "Because he hath found some uncleanness in her." Literally, the Hebrew says that he found in her "the nakedness of a thing."

a) "Uncleanness" interpreted

(1) By Jewish tradition

The Jews said that "uncleanness" could be any number of things: loose hair, spinning around in the street, saying bad things about your mother-in-law, burning the dinner, talking with men, and so on. That's what they interpreted as an uncleanness or indecency.

(2) By the context

The Bible mustn't be interpreted the way you want to interpret it; it's interpreted by its context. If you go backwards into the context of chapter 23, you will find the same term for "uncleanness" used in verse 14 in a regulation for dealing with physical elimination. Starting with verse 13 we read, "And thou shalt have a shovel among thy weapons; and it shall be, when thou wilt ease thyself abroad, thou shalt dig therewith, and shalt turn back and cover that which cometh from thee. For the Lord thy God walketh in the midst of thy camp, to deliver thee, and to give up thine enemies before thee; therefore shall thy camp be holy, that he see no unclean thing [or 'uncleanness, indecency'] in thee, and turn away from thee." It's simply saying, "Bury your excrement because God walks in your camp—along with a lot of other folks too." It was an obvious issue of decency.

The term for "uncleanness" in 24:1 is the same term as in 23:14. In other words, the man found some indecency in his wife—something unclean, dirty, vile, shameful, improper, unbecoming, and embarrassing to her husband.

41

b) "Uncleanness" investigated

The word "uncleanness" cannot refer to adultery. Why? Because adultery, at this point in Israel's history, resulted in death. Not only that, Moses wouldn't have used the word "uncleanness," he would have said adultery. It's referring to something dirty, embarrassing, or gross—but not adultery, because Deuteronomy 22:22–24 clearly says that the penalty for adultery is death. So whatever the uncleanness was, it was something short of adultery.

Nobody knows the exact identity of the uncleanness mentioned in Deuteronomy 24:1, but let me give you an idea as to its general character. If you knew that adultery ended in death, you might do a lot of things, but you would generally control yourself just short of adultery, true? So apparently there were people who were entering into shameless, indecent, habitual indulgence in sexual sin, but coming just short of actually committing adultery.

This appears to be what happened in Deuteronomy 24. This woman was probably shameful and vile but stopping short of adultery so that the death penalty couldn't be applied. And because of all these evil deeds, her husband divorced her. She then went out, married another man, and immediately became defiled. Why? Because there was no legitimate basis for her divorce. As soon as she entered into a relationship with another man, even though she had divorce papers in her hand, she was nothing but an adulteress.

You say, "It wasn't her fault! He dumped her." That's right. But he made her an adulteress nonetheless. In fact, in Matthew 5:32 Jesus says that if you divorce your wife for anything less than adultery, you make her an adulteress. So she became defiled. That's why husband number one couldn't take her back, even if her second husband died, because God didn't want him marrying a defiled adulteress.

The point, then, of Deuteronomy 24 is this: If you divorce your wife for anything short of adultery, you not only cause her to commit adultery, whoever marries her commits adultery. Then, when you remarry, you commit adultery and cause the woman you marry to commit adultery. In other words, you literally proliferate adultery.

Deuteronomy 24 does not command divorce. It commands a person not to remarry an illegitimately divorced person. It's a very strong word. If you marry an illegitimately divorced person, you're marrying someone who is defiled.

God is protecting marriage. You can't just divorce your wife for any reason you want, or you're going to turn her into an adulteress, whoever she marries into an adulterer, yourself into an adulterer, and whoever you marry into an adulteress. So remember that if you

42

ever think about getting rid of your wife. God is trying to insulate that one man-one woman, monogamous, lifelong relationship by making the alternative one of disaster. So this text commands that you do not remarry an illegitimately divorced person.

IV. THE AFFIRMATION (vv. 8-9)

A. The Permission of Moses (v. 8)

"He saith unto them, Moses, because of the hardness of your hearts, permitted you to put away [or 'divorce'] your wives, but from the beginning it was not so [or 'never intended to be']."

1. The restriction of his permission

Because of the hardness of their hearts, Moses permitted divorce—he tolerated it. But may I add that he didn't tolerate it for indecency or shameless behavior, so he wouldn't have tolerated it for anything less than that either. If he didn't tolerate it for vile behavior, he certainly didn't tolerate it for burning the dinner! If he didn't tolerate it for living on the thin edge of vice, adultery, and lewdness, he certainly wouldn't tolerate it because you found somebody nicer, because your wife talked to the wrong guy, or because you decided to go on to some other adventure. If it wasn't for something right on the edge of adultery, it wouldn't be for anything less than that.

So, Moses did permit divorce; but it wasn't in the Deuteronomy 24 passage. Frankly, the Old Testament doesn't say that Moses actually permitted divorce, but we know that he must have permitted it for a legitimate basis, or Deuteronomy 24 wouldn't have discussed the illegitimate basis. And since the Old Testament doesn't give us a text that says, "I permit you to get a divorce on the basis of so-and-so," we have to draw the principles out. I think there's a reason God avoided being specific in the Old Testament. It's a permission, but it's not overtly stated lest people hurry to that passage to justify themselves.

2. The reasons behind his permission

a) God's grace

The point of the Old Testament of this subject is this: Divorce for less than adultery leads to adultery. And when adultery occurred, it was punished by death. However, in God's grace there was a transition in the Old Testament from the death penalty for adultery to divorce. Because of His grace, God did not always enact the death penalty, did He? For example, did David commit adultery? Yes—many times. Was he put to death for it? No. Why? God was gracious. What about Solomon? Did he commit adultery? Only heaven could record the times (cf. 1 Kings 11:3).

Somewhere along the line, God in His tolerance spared life and allowed divorce. And if marriage could only be severed by death because of adultery, I'm convinced that God would

43

have only allowed marriage to be severed by divorce because of adultery as well.

b) Hard-hearted adultery

I believe that God especially permitted divorce in the case of hard-hearted adultery—which was an irreconcilable problem. In other words, if a wife was in an adulterous relationship which she would not sever, God may be gracious to her and not take her life. But God certainly would also permit the innocent party to divorce so that he would be free to remarry.

I believe that unrepentant, irreconcilable adultery constituted a hard heart. And in that case, Moses allowed divorce. He didn't condone it, commend it, or command it—he allowed it—and only when God was gracious and didn't bring death. That's all we can understand about it. Otherwise nothing makes sense. We cannot give any more latitude than the Word of God does. It was a concession on account of sin to make life more bearable for the one sinned against. God would not punish the innocent victim just because He was gracious enough to spare the life of the guilty one. If God killed the guilty one, the innocent one would be free to remarry, right? So just because God is gracious to the guilty one doesn't mean that He's going to penalize the innocent one.

So Moses allowed divorce, but according to verse 8, "from the beginning it was not so." Divorce was never God's original design—I hope you understand that. Deuteronomy 24 does not authorize divorce; it only stipulates no remarriage in the case of an illegitimate divorce. By the way, in Mark 10:3 Jesus speaks of Deuteronomy 24 as a command. But it's not a command to divorce; it's a command to not remarry a defiled partner. So don't be confused by that. Deuteronomy 24 is a prohibition for remarriage.

The Biblical Grounds for Divorce

The only biblical grounds for divorce would be adultery.

1.   Ezra 10:3–5

Verse 3 begins, "Now, therefore, let us make a covenant with our God to put away all the wives [the 'foreign women' of v. 2], and such as are born of them, according to the counsel of my lord, and of those who tremble at the commandment of our God; and let it be done according to the law." Here are the people of God saying, "Let's make a covenant with God to divorce our wives." Why? Because they had married pagan wives. God had forbidden them to do this, but they had entered into mixed marriages and had become spiritual adulterers. They had abandoned God and His commandments and had married those wives of adultery. There's a sense here in which God doesn't even recognize these marriages.

44

Continuing on in verses 4 and 5 they said to Ezra, "Arise; for this matter belongeth unto thee. We also will be with thee; be of good courage and do it. Then rose Ezra, and made the chief priests, the Levites, and all Israel, swear that they should do according to this word. And they swore."

There is actually an advocating of divorce here. The people are told that they should divorce. Now it's very difficult to interpret the specifics of this passage, but in general, what it's saying is this: They had entered into adulterous unions. In fact, if they had divorced their Jewish wives to marry these pagan women, God wouldn't have seen these pagan unions as legitimate unions. But even more than that, they had intermarried in spiritual adultery, and God saw divorce as legitimate in that case.

Let me go a step further. Pagan worship was adulterous. They had temple prostitutes, both male and female, and often engaged in sex orgies as a part of their worship. So I believe there was legitimate grounds for divorce here because their spouses were pagan adulterers and idolators. And on that basis, God was permitting them to shed their wives, or husbands, who were engaged in that incessant, unceasing worship of false gods connected not only with idolatry, but with adultery.

So implied in this passage, then, is that they were to be divorced because of spiritual intermarriage with idols and the physical union they were having with the prostitutes who carried on the idolatrous worship. This is a hint at the fact that there is legitimate divorce where there is adultery involved.

2. Isaiah 50:1a

In this particular verse, the Lord is confronting a wayward, disobedient, sinning people. Talking to them as a husband to a wife, the Lord says, "Where is the bill of your mother's divorcement, whom I have put away [or 'divorced']?' God says, "Where is your divorce certificate?" Of course, the answer is they don't have one. In other words, He's saying, "How dare you join yourselves to idols, how dare you commit spiritual adultery, how dare you abandon God and the worship of the true God, how dare you leave Me, your husband, O Israel, without a divorce? What gives you the right to do that? Have I divorced you?" The answer, of course, is that He had not.

3 Jeremiah 3:8a

Here in Jeremiah, God had been calling to Israel for seven hundred years. For seven hundred years He had been saying, "Stop your idolatry and your spiritual adultery." For seven hundred years Israel had been spiritually adulterous, incessantly joining themselves to other deities. So finally, after seven hundred years, God says, "And I saw, when for all the causes whereby backsliding Israel committed adultery I had put her away, and given her a bill of divorce." Who is that does the divorcing here? God! After seven hundred years of adultery, God divorced Israel.

The basis of a divorce in the Old Testament is adultery. The only way a marriage could be broken was through adultery. Why? Because if you committed adultery, you'd be dead— breaking the marriage and freeing the partner to remarry. However, if God was gracious and didn't take your life, divorce was permitted—primarily when there was a hardness of heart that could never be resolved. It took God seven hundred years to get to that place. So it's a great illustration of patience, isn't it? You don't say, "My husband did it once—that's the end of him!" Divorce should not occur unless it's in the case of continued hardness of heart.

So even God divorced. And that's important, because God does not do things that aren't right. God doesn't give us living illustrations of His own behavior that we can't follow. That's why it grieves me that people will come along and say, "There are no grounds for divorce." There is—adultery—especially a prolonged, unrepentant, irreconcilable case of adultery.

4.   Jeremiah 31:31–32

"Behold, the days come, saith the Lord, that I will make a new covenant with the house of Israel, and with the house of Judah." Do you know what He's going to do? He's going to get married again—to Israel. Verse 32 says, "Not according to the covenant that I made with their fathers in the day that I took them by the hand to bring them out of the land of Egypt, which, my covenant, they broke, although I was an husband unto them, saith the Lord." Now that affirms that God was no longer their husband, doesn't it? But He will remarry them and make a new covenant.

5.   Matthew 1:18–19

Verse 18 says, "Now the birth of Jesus Christ was in this way: When, as his mother, Mary, was espoused to Joseph, before they came together [i.e., before they had any sexual relationship at all], she was found with child of the Holy Spirit." You can imagine the shock that Joseph must have had. He must have been shattered to find out that such a woman of virtue, such a pure child of God as his beloved Mary, could ever be pregnant illegitimately.

Now the key is in verse 19, "Then Joseph, her husband, being a just [or 'righteous'] man, and not willing to make her a public example, was minded to put her away [or 'divorce her'] privately." Joseph was a righteous man, and he was going to divorce his wife. Now that tells us there *is* a just cause for divorce, doesn't it? He didn't do it. However, because of the purity of his own heart and soul, it was traumatic for Joseph to deal with having a wife whom he thought had consummated a union in which she was impregnated with an illegitimate child. So his first reaction as a righteous man was to no longer continue his marriage to a defiled woman.

Why did divorce replace the death penalty for adultery?

1. The grace of God

   I've already suggested this, but one reason why divorce replaced death is the grace of God. It's the same reason, in the early years of the church, Ananias and Sapphira died for not giving what they promised to the Lord, yet other folks throughout the history of the church have done the same thing and haven't died. God was establishing examples then, but now He is more patient with us.

2. The lack of national righteousness

   Another reason why the death penalty wasn't enforced was possibly because there wasn't anybody around pure enough to enforce it. All of the executioners would have to kill themselves first, because the nation was so filled with adultery. In fact, this is exactly the point that Jesus made in John 8:7b, when the Pharisees brought to Him a woman caught in the act of adultery. He said, "He that is without sin among you, let him first cast a stone at her." It's possible He was saying, "You're a bunch of adulterers yourselves. How dare you be such hypocrites!"

God never intended divorce for any reason. But where there was adultery, God had the guilty partner killed. That's how sacred marriage is! You would die if you committed adultery. But because God was gracious and men were sinful, God permitted divorce where there was a case of constant, irreconcilable adultery. This Old Testament permission was only designed to meet unique, practical problems in an imperfect, sinful world.

Adultery was the only thing that could break the bond of marriage—either by death or divorce. And since divorce was a merciful concession to the adulterer, can we then say that God would penalize the innocent party by not allowing remarriage? In the Old Testament, if your husband committed adultery, he was killed, right? He had no chance to repent. Well, would you be free to remarry? Sure, because death breaks the marriage. But if God allows divorce instead of death, would He penalize the innocent person to a life of celibacy? Hardly! He wouldn't be gracious to the guilty and make the innocent pay the price. So I believe that where there are grounds for divorce, there must also be grounds for remarriage. After all, the purpose of divorce was only to show mercy to the guilty, not to sentence the innocent to lifelong singleness, loneliness, or misery.

47

B. The Proliferation of Adultery (v. 9)

"And I say unto you, Whosoever shall put away [or 'divorce'] his wife, except it be for fornication, and shall marry another, committeth adultery; and whosoever marrieth her who is put away [or 'divorced'] doth commit adultery."

The word "fornication" (Gk., *porneia*) is commonly used to encompass adultery. For example, 1 Corinthians 10:8 says, "Neither let us commit fornication [Gk., *porneia*], as some of them committed, and fell in one day three and twenty thousand." Now people say, "It's talking about fornication there, not adultery. It's referring to sex outside of marriage." They're saying, then, that all twenty-three thousand people who were killed by God were unmarried. That's silly! Obviously, the word encompasses both sex outside of marriage and sex that would be constituted as adultery. Paul is not just referring only to unmarried Israelites or unmarried Corinthians. The word encompasses all sexual evil.

1. The principle repeated by Jesus

Here in verse 9, Jesus basically says the same thing that He said in Matthew 5:31–32: When you get a divorce for any reason other than adultery, you proliferate more adultery. So verse 9 is not a new thought or truth, it's Matthew 5 as well as Deuteronomy 24 all over again.

2. The principle reaffirmed by Paul

In 1 Corinthians 7:10–11, Paul fills in our thinking a little bit. He says, "And unto the married I command, yet not I, but the Lord, Let not the wife depart from her husband." Now here Paul reaffirms the same basic truth, Don't leave your husband. Then he says, "But and if she depart, let her remain unmarried." Why? Because she has no basis at all to remarry. If she does, she'll become an adulteress. However, she has a second option, "or be reconciled to her husband; and let not the husband put away [or 'divorce'] his wife." So stay married! That's very, very important.

Jesus upheld God's ideal and silenced the Pharisees. In fact He made them appear as adulterers. Every time they came to Him they really walked into a buzz saw. They were trying to discredit Jesus, but before the conversation was half over, they were standing there in the public's gaze, accused and convicted adulterers.

No, divorce is not God's will for every cause. It is never His will for any cause. It is only permitted in the case of adultery—primarily prolonged and unrepentant adultery.

The Biblical Affirmation of Remarriage

The Bible affirms the right to remarry.

In Cases of Death

1. Romans 7:3—"So, then if, while her husband liveth, she be married to another man, she shall be called an adulteress; but

if her husband be dead, she is free from that law, so that she is no adulteress, though she be married to another man." In other words, remarriage is OK under certain circumstances—one of which is the death of a spouse.

2. 1 Timothy 5:14—"I will, therefore, that the younger women [or 'widows'; see v. 11] marry, bear children, rule the house, give no occasion to the adversary to speak reproachfully." Young widows are called on to remarry. So remarriage is OK!

3. 1 Corinthians 7:39—"The wife is bound by the law as long as her husband liveth; but if her husband be dead, she is at liberty to be married to whom she will, only in the Lord."

In Cases of Divorce

If God permits remarriage when there is death, then in cases of adultery when God went by the absolute nature of His law and death occurred, there would always be the possibility of remarriage, right? And just because God allows for divorce when there can be no reconciliation, that doesn't mean that the innocent party has to remain single for the rest of his life. I believe that God allows remarriage in the case of a divorce caused by adultery.

Look what Paul says in 1 Corinthians 7:27–28a, "Art thou bound unto a wife? Seek not to be loosed. Art thou loosed from a wife [i.e., Have you been divorced]? Seek not a wife. But and if thou marry, thou hath not sinned." In other words, if you have been loosed from a wife (it doesn't say how), and it is justified, legitimate, and according to biblical grounds, if you marry, you have not sinned.

God permits remarriage where divorce is on biblical grounds.

Focusing on the Facts

1. Why doesn't a sexual relationship constitute a marriage? What does constitute a marriage (see pp. 38–39)?

2. When the Pharisees asked Jesus about Moses' "command" to divorce, were they interested in the divine ideal that the Lord had just presented? What were they interested in? Why then did they ask their question (see p. 39)?

3. What passage of Scripture were the Pharisees referring to when they asked about Moses' "command" to divorce (see pp. 39–40)?

4. Why is the "first husband" of Deuteronomy 24:1–4 not allowed to remarry his first wife (see p. 40)?

5. Did Moses give a command to divorce? What *does* Deuteronomy 24:1–4 command? How does the KJV translation obscure this idea (see pp. 40–41)?

6. According to Deuteronomy 24:1 why did the man divorce his wife? What is the literal Hebrew interpretation of the word "uncleanness"? What

49

was the traditional Jewish interpretation of this word? How should it be interpreted in its context (see pp. 40–42)?

7. Why can't the word "uncleanness" refer to adultery? Apparently, what "uncleanness" was this woman involved in (see p. 42)?

8. Even though the woman in Deuteronomy 24 had divorce papers in her hand, why wasn't she to remarry? What did she become when she did remarry? Why (see p. 42)?

9. What is the overall lesson of Deuteronomy 24:1–4 (see pp. 42–43)?

10. Did Moses permit divorce? What Old Testamant text supports this? How do we know that Moses permitted divorce (see p. 43)?

11. What's one good reason why God probably avoided giving an overt statement detailing Moses's permission of divorce in Scripture (see p. 43)?

12. If the penalty for adultery in the Old Testament was death, why weren't people like David and Solomon killed (see p. 43)?

13. In a situation where hard-hearted adultery wasn't punished by death, why was it necessary for God to permit divorce (see p. 44)?

14. If God took the life of an adulterer, would the innocent party be free to remarry? Why must this also be true if God spared the life of the adulterer and permitted divorce instead (see p. 44)?

15. According to Matthew 19:8, how do we know that divorce is not God's intention for marriage (see p. 44)?

16. What were the details behind Ezra's command for the people of God to divorce their wives? Why was this legitimate (see pp. 44–45; Ezra 10:3–5)?

17. Who wrote Israel a bill of divorcement in Jeremiah 3:8? Why (see pp. 45–46)?

18. If your marriage partner commits adultery and then repents of it, do you think God would want you to divorce? Explain (see p. 46).

19. Does God stay permanently divorced from Israel? Support your answer (see p. 46).

20. What is significant about Joseph's desire to divorce Mary when he found out she was pregnant (see pp. 46–47)?

21. Why did divorce replace the death penalty for adultery in the Old Testament (see p. 47)?

22. If there are legitimate grounds for divorce, why must there also be legitimate grounds for remarriage (see p. 47)?

23. What does the word "fornication" in Matthew 19:9 mean? How is this word used in 1 Corinthians 10:8? Why must this word encompass adultery (see p. 48)?

24. Matthew 19:9 is basically a repeat of what previous text in Matthew? Where does Paul reaffirm these truths (see p. 48)?

25. What New Testament texts affirm the right to remarry in the event a partner dies? In the event of a divorce (see p. 49)?

Pondering the Principles

1. The Pharisees were only interested in finding loopholes in the law of God to accommodate their sin. Are there any sins in your life that you are trying to excuse or justify because of some technical "loophole"? Read Psalm 139:23–24 and let the Lord show you the areas that you are falling short in. Then confess those sins to Him.

2. If your spouse went out and committed adultery, what would your reaction be? What should your reaction be, based on the example of Hosea and Gomer and of God and Israel? Memorize Malachi 2:16*a*, " 'For I hate divorce' says the Lord, the God of Israel" (NASB).

4

Jesus' Teaching on Divorce—
Part 4

Outline

Review
I. The Attack
II. The Answer
III. The Argument
IV. The Affirmation

Lesson
V. The Appropriation
  A. The Disciples' Reaction
    1. Their perception of marriage
    2. The biblical perception of marriage
      a) Proverbs 5:15–19
      b) Proverbs 18:22
      c) Proverbs 19:14*b*
      d) 1 Peter 3:7*b*
    3. Today's perception of marriage
      a) The problem of pursuing romantic feelings
        (1) It is short-lived
        (2) It is fickle
      b) The potential of pursuing true love
  B. Jesus' Response
    1. The capacity to receive His words
      a) Conditions for singleness
      b) Categories of singleness
        (1) Congenital reasons
        (2) Castration
        (3) Commitment to God
    2. The command to receive His words

Introduction

Matthew 19:1–12 contains our Lord's teaching on the subject of divorce—a very pertinent subject today. We've been examining exactly what the Lord says in this text because it's important for our understanding of God's will relative to divorce and remarriage.

Now keep in mind that the first two verses of chapter 19 gave us the setting. The Lord had finished the discourse on the childlikeness of the believer in

52

chapter 18—ending His Galilean ministry. Then in chapters 19 and 20, He moved into His Perean ministry. This ministry was much like the Galilean ministry—only it was much briefer. No doubt, the majority of the people did not believe in Him—but some did.

So as the Perean ministry begins, Jesus is confronted in verse 3 by His archenemies, the Pharisees. They were totally intimidated by Him and His teaching because both He and what He said were so contrary to them. They began by asking Him a question with which they wanted to trap Him.

Review

I. THE ATTACK (v. 3; see pp. 7–10)

Testing Jesus, the Pharisees asked Him, "Is it lawful for a man to put away his wife for every cause?"

II. THE ANSWER (vv. 4–6; see pp. 10–15, 20–33)

Jesus answered the Pharisees—but not on His own. He quoted God by going all the way back to Genesis 1:27 and 2:24. In verse 4 Jesus says, "Have ye not read?" as if to say, "Your argument isn't with Me, your argument is with God!" He then proceeded to show them that God intends for marriage to be: one man for one woman—for life, a strong bond, indivisibly one flesh, and an act of God that is never to be divorced.

Well, they anticipated that Jesus would take this hard line, so they had a second question ready to confront Him with. That takes us to the next point.

III. THE ARGUMENT (v. 7; see pp. 39–43)

The Pharisees' argument was as follows: "Why did Moses then command to give a writing of divorcement, and to put her away?" In other words, "If God laid down a 'no divorce' standard in the very beginning, then why did Moses command divorce?" Well, in our last lesson we discussed this and saw that they had twisted Deuteronomy 24:1–4. Moses did *not* command divorce! The only command in the text is to not marry a defiled adulteress. There is no command to get a divorce. Moses simply tolerated divorce.

IV. THE AFFIRMATION (vv. 8–9; see pp. 43–49)

Jesus acknowledged Moses' toleration of divorce and then reaffirmed the divine standard: "Moses, because of the hardness of your hearts, permitted you to put away your wives, but from the beginning it was not so. And I say unto you, Whosoever shall put away his wife, except it be for fornication, and shall marry another, committeth adultery; and whosoever marrieth her who is put away doth commit adultery." In other words, Jesus reiterated the one Old Testament grounds for divorce, adultery, which comes under the broad category of fornication or sexual sin.

Remember, divorce was never commanded. If a person committed adultery and then repented of it, he was to be forgiven and restored in

53

love—just as God will take back His adulterous wife, Israel, and as Hosea bought back his adulterous wife, Gomer. However, in the case of hard-hearted adultery in which a person would not turn and repent, divorce was an option—it was permitted. Why? As a merciful concession to the innocent party. You see, if God had killed the adulterer, the innocent party would have been free to remarry anyway. So if God by His grace spares the life of the guilty, then you can see how reasonable it is that divorce should free the innocent party to remarry. "But divorce on any other grounds," says our Lord, "causes the people who remarry after that divorce to turn into adulterers and adulteresses—defiling them all!"

At this point, the Pharisees disappear. Why? Because they had just been exposed as the adulterers that they were. Since they had divorced for reasons other than adultery—perhaps a myriad of times—they had to face the reality that they were nothing more than a bunch of adulterers. So they fade from the scene. But by this time, the disciples are literally enraptured with this teaching of our Lord, and the scene moves into a house (Mark 10:10).

In verse 10, the Lord sits down with the disciples and follows up on His discussion about marriage. I wish we had that discussion. If there's any one category of truth that I'd like to have more of in the Bible, it would be about divorce and remarriage. However, the discussion isn't recorded—only the disciples' response.

Here's the scene: The disciples are in the house, gathered around the Lord. The strength of His teaching about marriage and divorce has left a tremendous impression on them. In fact, they're actually shocked by it. You see, Jesus had not extended the Old Testament law one whit. He simply reaffirmed it—no divorce. Frankly, if God killed all adulterers with the capital punishment that He assigns in Leviticus 20:10, there would never be any divorce. But God in His grace has let some adulterers live. So divorce can be a merciful concession, primarily when that adultery is hard-hearted and irreconcilable. There's still a place for forgiveness when there's repentance, but divorce for any reason other than adultery is forbidden.

The disciples, then, are very curious about Jesus' teaching. Why? Because they had grown up in a culture where divorce was rampant—a culture very much like ours. All that the Lord has said must have left them struggling.

Lesson

V. THE APPROPRIATION (vv. 10–12)

How do these men appropriate this truth about divorce to themselves? How do they handle this? Well, it really provoked their thinking because it was totally foreign to the experience of their day and the way they had been taught. For example, they were raised in a culture where divorce was actually a virtue. Let me quote from some of the Talmudic writing of the rabbis. "Among those who will never behold the face of hell is he who has a bad wife. Such a man is saved from hell because he has expiated his sins on earth." "A bad wife is like leprosy to her husband. What is the remedy? Let him divorce her and be cured of his leprosy." "If a man has a bad wife, it is a religious duty to divorce her.

Could you imagine your children being raised under the teaching that if you get a bad wife, divorce her? Well, that's what the disciples were taught. So, when the Lord comes along and says, "Only in the case of adultery will God mercifully concede a divorce," the disciples recognize the obvious tension between what they're hearing from the Lord and what they've experienced in their society. The disparity is so great that they are completely nonplussed. When they heard this very narrow, hard standard, they had a definite reaction.

A. The Disciples' Reaction (v. 10)

"His disciples say unto him, If the case of the man be so with his wife, it is not good to marry."

1. Their perception of marriage

Do you understand what the disciples are saying? They are saying, "Boy, if you get into a marriage and you can't get out of it, you'd be better off never to get into it! To be tied to a wife that only her adultery could release, and then to be compelled to put up with all the rest of her idiosyncrasies, short of adultery, would be next to impossible. What if she's strange or doesn't make you happy? You'd be stuck for the rest of your life. Forget it! You're better off to stay single."

Well, they perceived fairly well what the Lord was saying, didn't they? They really did. However, may I suggest to you that they were not necessarily right? It isn't necessarily better to be single.

There are a lot of people who are like them today. They avoid marriage because they're not ready to make a lifetime commitment. Have you noticed that? They just want to flit from one romance to another—without any lasting commitment. Well, these people forfeit the richest meaning in life—a true relationship of love that lasts a lifetime—and settle for a cheap counterfeit.

2. The biblical perception of marriage

a) Proverbs 5:15–19—"Drink waters out of thine own cistern, and running waters out of thine own well." In other words, have your own wife. "Let thy fountains [the ability to procreate] be dispersed abroad, and rivers of waters in the streets. Let them be only thine own, and not for strangers with thee." In other words, procreation is only to be with your wife. "Let thy fountain be blessed, and rejoice with the wife of thy youth. Let her be as the loving hind and pleasant roe; let her breasts satisfy thee at all times, and be thou ravished always with her love." We see that marriage is marvelous, wonderful, and thrilling. It's good, blessed, God-given, and God-ordained.

b) Proverbs 18:22—"Whoso findeth a wife findeth a good thing, and obtaineth favor from the Lord."

c) Proverbs 19:14*b*—"A prudent wife is from the Lord."

d) 1 Peter 3:7*b*—"Being heirs together of the grace of life."

3. Today's perception of marriage

When the disciples said, "It is not good to marry," they were reflecting a pretty common attitude. They were saying, "Boy, if once I get into a marriage I have to stay there the rest of my life, and I can't get out of it—I'm never going to get into it!" Well, we have that same kind of mentality today, don't we? The reason people are not willing to marry and the reason marriages don't last is that people don't get married for the right reasons. They don't get married to make commitments. They don't get married out of an understanding of virtue and character.

a) The problem of pursuing romantic feelings

Dorothy Tennov, in a book called *Love and Limerence,* coins the word *limerence,* that is supposed to be a word to describe the bells that ring when you go through the stupor of romantic feelings. In our society people look for one emotion after another. They're pursuing romantic feelings but not real romance in the true sense. This book shows a series of sociological tests and surveys on the subject of romantic feeling. (They call it love, but I call it romantic feeling!) The book's conclusion is this:

(1) It is short-lived

This book concludes that all giddy, romantic emotion dies. It all dies and will always die. If you've been married for a long time, you realize that you no longer feel about your partner the way you did when you had the euphoria of romantic emotion at the beginning of your relationship. From time to time it recurs, but it's not there as it was in the beginning.

(2) It is fickle

People make relationships on the high euphoria of romantic feeling. However, when they lose that feeling, they go on to someone else. It's all short-lived and fickle. People hop from one romantic emotion to another. When they're with a person for awhile and the relationship starts to settle, all it takes is for someone else to come across their path who attracts them. Then once the romantic emotions are triggered, they dump their old partner and run over to the new one. People go through life doing that until they have burned off everything they ever could have had in terms of genuine feelings. They end up alone with nothing but emptiness.

That's the way the world lives, isn't it? They won't come to marriage with commitment. So they flit from one romance to

56

another. The result is what we see in our society today—the saddest of which is a generation of disoriented, unloved, lonely, isolated kids who are turning into criminals and misfits. Why? Because they don't have any meaningful long-term relationship to identify with. It's really tragic!

If you get married for an emotional feeling, you're making a big, big mistake. Now, there should be some of that there, but you better be able to see beyond that to virtue and character. You better understand that you will be sharing common spiritual values and common life values, and that you are making a lifelong, one man-one woman, strong-bond, one-flesh, God-made, no-divorce union. That's God's plan, but people in our society don't understand that at all.

b) The potential of pursuing true love

I heard a speaker recently who was relating to a women's liberation group the story of a particular gentleman in the ministry who had been married for nearly fifty years. He was relating the story of the death of this man's wife to illustrate the difference between true love and romance. He said that one morning this man and his wife were eating breakfast as they had done for years and years. She ate her breakfast and then fell over onto the table. Immediately scooping up her body, he ran out the door, put her delicately into the car, and then sped to the hospital. By the time he got there, she was dead. Well, you have to be with somebody that you love for nearly fifty years to understand the emptiness that he felt. He knew, of course, that she was with the Lord Jesus Christ, which is where his devotion was.

After the memorial service had taken place at the graveside, the man and his sons got into their car and started home. Suddenly, the man said, "Stop! I have to go back." Stopping the car, his sons said, "Look, Dad, we don't want you to go back. It's too much for you. You don't need any more sorrow. We need to just go on." But the man said, "No, I have to go back—I have to go back."

Unable to argue him out of going back, they turned around and took him back to the grave. When they got there, he went out to the grave, knelt down and patted it, and then stood there for a few moments. Returning to the car, he said, "Now it's all right, we can go." On their way home he said to his sons, "This is a good day—a wonderful day. This is just the way I wanted it to be." "What do you mean?" his sons asked. "Oh," he said, "I always wanted her to go first—always. So, this is a good day."

The man who was relating this story to the women's group then said, "Listen, anybody who knows the meaning of true love always wants the other person to go first, because they

57

don't want them to endure the pain, sorrow, anxiety of loneliness, and the burial of the one they have loved." Then he said, "I daresay that your romantic relationships are a far cry from that kind of feeling and reality." He was right!

You see, people settle for a cheap substitute for the rich, deepening, profound, thrilling, meaningful friendship that two souls knit together in love can experience as years go on. And the disciples needed to hear what people today need to hear. Marriage is a lifelong commitment—which is not a reason to avoid it; it's a reason to get into it. In the genuineness of that lifelong friendship, God will bless you in ways you will never experience as a single person—never.

The Criteria for Evaluating a Potential Marriage Partner

I don't know what some of you single people are looking for, but it seems to me that some of you ought to be looking to get into marriage rather than retreating back from it. And you ought to start having different criteria to evaluate people. You should start seeing beyond the advertisements and the Hollywood glamor and begin looking for real character. And once you find a godly person with whom you share common values in Jesus Christ, and with whom you can build a deep, profound, and meaningful companionship of life, then you'd better grab onto that opportunity. Personally, I believe that God will give you some emotions that will make you happy and thrill you too. But there had better be more than just that.

You see, the disciples, like so many people today, missed the point. You ought to rush to get into a lifelong relationship. However, the disciples were right in this regard—you don't want to get into marriage with the wrong person. So when you make that move, you'd better be sure you're looking for spiritual values. And you'd better be sure you're getting involved with someone whose spiritual commitments are as deep and as far and as wide as yours are. And if you don't know that yet, you'd better slow down the process. Otherwise, you may spend your whole life individually trying to keep the relationship together. And that's tough—very tough.

So on the one hand, find someone with like precious faith and like values who loves Jesus Christ and has a life goal the same as yours and see if God might not bring you together. But on the other hand, if you find someone you want to marry fast, and she doesn't have those values, you'd better back off. Marriage is a sacred thing—the greatest gift that God could ever give to two people. And I can tell you from my own experience that when you have two people who love Jesus Christ, and love each other, and live a life together under God's leading and direction in the power of the Spirit, it gets so good sometimes, you have to pinch yourself to see if it's real. That's how God intended it!

So instead of saying, "Hey, I'm never going to get married if I'm going to get stuck with the same person for the rest of my life," say, "Now, if that's the case, I want to get married, because it's God's ordained plan. However, I want it with the right person so that I don't get stuck for the rest of my life. I want to find a person who has character, not just someone who makes me feel romantic emotions." You see, the truth of the matter is this: If you get married for romantic emotions, you'll be a basket case for the rest of your life. Why? Because those romantic feelings will continue to spring up as certain people come across your path. If that's all you have going for you when you get married, you will be dead in the water before you start. Your marriage will never last.

B. Jesus' Response (vv. 11–12)

　1. The capacity to receive His words (vv. 11–12a)

　　a) Conditions for singleness (v. 11)

"But he said unto them, All men cannot receive this saying, except they to whom it is given."

What "saying" is He talking about? The saying of the previous verse, "If the case of the man be so with his wife, it is not good to marry." He says, "That's a nice idea. If you just stay single, you won't get into something that you can't get out of. But not everybody can handle singleness. Only those to whom it is given." May I suggest to you that singleness is a gift, of sorts. Singleness is given to a person. That's what Jesus is saying. And unless you can handle singleness, it isn't going to be the best thing for you. You may say, "I don't want to get married because I don't want to make a commitment." But all you're going to be left with is a roller coaster of emotions, as you find yourself being tempted with all kinds of illicit thoughts (if not acts as well) for the rest of your life.

Some people who ought to have been married long ago are still single—not because they shouldn't get married or because there isn't somebody to marry, but because they're probably concentrating on looks instead of character. Not only that, it's possible that they themselves are not yet the right person. Therefore the other right person can't recognize them. So we ought to be looking for marriage. It's the norm. That's what our Lord means when He says, "Not everybody can be single. Only those to whom it has been given." Not everybody can handle that!

By the way, the word "receive" in verse 11 is an interesting word. It basically means "to have room or space for something." Its metaphorical use is to embrace something with heart and mind. So not everybody can handle being single. I've had people say to me, "You would have probably been able to serve the Lord more effectively if you were single. You'd have been free to go here and there, without having to

59

take care of your wife and four kids.'' Well, that's probably true. There's a sense in which if I'd been single, I would have had more liberty to do certain things. However I'm not the kind of person who can receive being single. God knows that! Frankly, that's the way it is with most people. God made us for marriage.

b) Categories of singleness (v. 12a)

(1) Congenital reasons

"For there are some eunuchs [those who do not engage in sexual activity], who were so born from their mother's womb.''

We would say this is singleness due to congenital reasons. There are some people who are born with underdeveloped or malformed sexual organs. So, they don't have the capability or the desire to function sexually. These people can handle being single.

(2) Castration

"And there are some eunuchs, who were made eunuchs by men.''

This is talking about castration. In ancient history, the people who were chosen out of society to work in harems were castrated so that they wouldn't go beyond the bounds of what they should do in that environment. There were also religious pagans who felt that castration was a way to please their gods. So, people who have castrated themselves, or had themselves castrated, can't function in a marriage either.

(3) Commitment to God

"And there are eunuchs, who have made themselves eunuchs for the kingdom of heaven's sake.''

Now this isn't referring to physical surgery, it's referring to dedication and commitment to God. In other words, there are some people who are single for God's sake.

It's interesting to me that these are the only categories of singleness. There are those who cannot marry and engage themselves in a normal physical union because of a hereditary congenital defect; there are those who cannot because of some accident or act at the hands of men; and then there are those who are single for the kingdom of heaven's sake. Notice that there isn't anybody in those categories who is single because he can't be bothered to make a commitment he can't get out of. Why? Because that doesn't solve anything. It just leaves a person in a state of singleness, where he is faced with the greater problem of trying to handle his desires.

Notice the last group for a moment: those that are single for the kingdom of heaven's sake. In 1 Corinthians 7:7 Paul talks about singleness as a "gift of God." This gift is to be used for the glory of God in the service of Christ. Now let me say this to all of you that are single: If you feel your singleness is from God because you don't sense a need to marry, and because you sense the Spirit of God leading you into service to Christ as a single person, that is good—very good. In fact, I believe if you got Paul into a corner, he'd say that it's better to be single. Why? Because you're free to give your life in service to Christ (1 Cor. 7:32–35). However, that's the only reason—beyond the two physical reasons—for singleness.

The Bible doesn't allow us to avoid marriage because of the commitment. It's only permitted if we physically can't marry or if we choose not to marry for the sake of the kingdom in service to Christ. I've been on mission fields in remote parts of the world where I've seen God uniquely use single people to whom He has given the gift of singleness. I've also seen people in our own local church who have been gifted by the Spirit of God for single ministry to Jesus Christ. Their unique gift brings wonderful blessings upon the Body of Jesus Christ. I'd never want them to change. However, if you're a single person just trying to overcome the desire for marriage, then perhaps your singleness is not a gift from God. If that's the case, you ought to begin to seek marriage and to open your heart to one of like precious faith and common value.

2. The command to receive His words (v. 12*b*)

At the end of verse 12 the Lord says, "He that is able to receive it, let him receive it." Receive what? All His teachings about marriage and singleness. If you're married, you're to stay married for life; and if you're single, you're to stay single only if you're physically or spiritually disposed to singleness by a gift given to those who are to serve God in a unique way. However, marriage is the norm.

I think the Lord's statement at the end of verse 12 about receiving what He had to say is very important. You see, the Lord says this because He knows that most people aren't going to be able to receive it. For example, if I went into a local college classroom and said, "Here's God's standard: You will marry one person and stay with that person for the rest of your life—a lifetime commitment with no divorce. Furthermore, if you are single, remain single for the kingdom of God, and never play around." How well do you think I would be received? They'd probably say, "Who is this idiot? Where'd he come from?" Do you see the point? They wouldn't be able to receive God's standards.

This, in fact, happened to me some years back when I was invited to speak on a university campus on the subject of Christian sex ethics. I started out saying that none of them would be

61

able to accept any of what I was going to say. Well, when you say that to college students, their immediate reaction will be, "Oh, yeah?" putting them right where I wanted them. One student said, "Well, why won't we be able to accept what you say?" I replied, "Because you do not love the Lord Jesus Christ, the Bible has no authority in your life. What it says will be meaningless to you until you come to know and love the Lord Jesus Christ." He replied, "Well, how do I do that, then?" At that point, I was able to present the gospel to the entire class—which is really what I wanted to do anyway!

Do you see the point? God hasn't called me to straighten up the sexual antics of a pagan society. They're not even interested in the principles of God. My message is not to the world; it's to those who can receive the things of God—to believers in Christ. So what Jesus is saying is this, "If you have the ability to receive My sayings, you'd better receive them." In other words, if you have the life of God in your soul, if you love the Lord Jesus Christ, and if you are under the authority of the Word of God, you'd better receive this teaching. What teaching? The teaching that says that you're married for life, or you're single for the glory of God or for some physical reason. You're not to be single just so that you can play around without ever making a commitment.

I'll never understand why people want to cheat themselves out of the blessedness of marriage, the deep and meaningful friendship that occurs as two souls are knit together in love, the friendship that knows absolutely no limitations, no bounds, no inhibitions—the truest kind of friendship that expresses the deepest kind of love through caring and the sharing of everything. If you never know this in life, you will have cheated yourself. The cheap thrills that you look for on the shallow end of relationships will never buy you that—never.

So as Christians, of all people, we should be hearing and receiving these sayings of Jesus. When you enter into a marriage, understand that because you're going into it for life, you'd better be marrying for something beyond your feelings.

Six Reasons for Marriage

1. Procreation

   In Genesis 1:28 God brought a man and a woman together, married them, and told them to fill and replenish the earth. Psalm 127:3–5a says, "Lo, children are an heritage from the Lord; and the fruit of the womb is his reward. As arrows are in the hand of a mighty man, so are children of one's youth. Happy is the man who hath his quiver full of them." God created marriage for procreation.

   Did you know that over thirty-five percent of all married couples who are of childbearing age have been permanently sterilized?

People don't want kids intruding into their lives. Why? Because they are in romantic love and they want to be able to flit from one relationship to another. For them, kids become a longlasting problem.

But God designed children to bind a marriage together. Nothing shows that two people are one more clearly than when they see themselves in the child born of their union.

Marriage is for procreation. And that doesn't mean you're to have children and then send them off to a day-care center, where they shove your kids into a room and "take care of them" while you do whatever it is you do. *You're* to take care of them and raise them, not some surrogate. That's part of the responsibility of marriage.

2. Pleasure

Marriage is also for pleasure. Hebrews 13:4a says, "Marriage is honorable in all, and the bed undefiled." You can't do anything in the marriage bed that is defiling. First Corinthians 7:4 says that the husband's body is his wife's, and the wife's body is her husband's. They both belong to each other! The Old Testament also talks about the satisfaction and pleasure of the physical relationship of marriage (e.g., Prov. 5:18–19; Song of Solomon). Marriage is for pleasure.

3. Purity

In 1 Corinthians 7:2a, Paul says, "Nevertheless, to avoid fornication, let every man have his own wife." Marriage is for purity.

4. Provision

Ephesians 5:25–33 says that the husband is to nourish, cherish, provide for, care for, and be like a savior to his wife. In marriage, all the women running around loose are to be scooped up and provided for—one at a time, however. That's what the Bible teaches. Marriage is a provision of security, caring, nourishing, and cherishing. In fact, 1 Timothy 5:8 says that if a man doesn't provide for his own household, he's worse than an unbeliever. Marriage is a provision for the care of the "weaker vessel" (1 Pet. 3:7), so that she can fulfill herself in childbearing and the companionship of marriage.

5. Partnership

When God made Eve, He said He made for Adam a helper— somebody to come alongside. In marriage, you don't do things alone; you do them together. And there's strength in that fellowship, isn't there? I confess to you that my wife is strong where I am weak, and I tend to be strong where she is weak. That's the way it's supposed to be. There's to be a real partnership in marriage. For example, while I'm studying and doing all the things I need to do, my wife is at home caring for all the needs of the home and the children. She frees me to do what God has called me to do. And I provide for her all the resources that she needs to do what God has ordained for her to do. It's a real partnership.

6. Picture

According to Ephesians 5:22–33, marriage is a picture of Christ and His church. It's a graphic demonstration in the face of the world that God has an ongoing, unending relationship with the bride whom He loves, and for whom He died and forever lives. Unfortunately, the whole metaphor of marriage as a symbol of Christ and His church has lost its punch, because the church is so rife with divorce and fouled-up marriages. It's sad, because the marriage metaphor is such a marvelous way to illustrate God's relationship to His church.

So God ordained marriage for procreation, pleasure, purity, provision, partnership, and as a picture of His relationship to His church. God ordained that marriage should be lifelong, full of love, blessed, and fulfilling. It is to be "the grace of life," as Peter calls it. Believe me, that's no reason to stay out of marriage—that's reason to get into it. But make sure that when you do get married, you get married for the right reason and with the right person. In time, looks won't matter anymore, but character and value will go right on through to the end. Be single if God has physically made you that way or if you're that way because of a gift of serving the kingdom. And if Christ is in control of your life, you are able to receive this teaching—so receive it!

A psychologist did a study and came up with a theory that you are what you are because you're adjusting to the most important person in your life. And the one you're trying to please is the most important person in your life. Well, for the Christian that's very simple, isn't it? Who is the most important person in our lives? Jesus Christ! And that settles the issue, really, because now we can say to Him, "I receive it, if You say it." That's God's order.

Focusing on the Facts

1. How did the disciples react to Jesus' teaching on divorce? Why (see pp. 54–55)?

2. What conclusion about marriage did the disciples make in Matthew 19:10? Was their conclusion right? Explain (see pp. 55–56).

3. What perspective do the following verses give regarding marriage: Proverbs 5:15–19; 18:22; 19:14b (see pp. 55–56)?

4. What are the two major problems of pursuing romantic feelings (see p. 56)?

5. What will eventually occur in marriages that are based on romantic feelings? What effects will this have on the next generation (see pp. 56–57)?

6. After many years of marriage, why would true love want the other person to die first (see pp. 57–58)?

7. What are the proper criteria for evaluating a potential marriage partner? What criteria do the world use (see pp. 58–59)?

8. Why is it so important to marry the right person (see p. 59)?

9. Should people try to stay single as long as they possibly can? Why or why not (see p. 59)?

10. In looking for the right person to marry, why is it important to concentrate on your own character as well (see p. 59)?

11. If being single gives a person more freedom to serve the Lord more effectively, why shouldn't all people in the ministry be single (see pp. 59–60)?

12. What three categories of singleness does Jesus mention in Matthew 19:12? Are there any other categories besides these three (see p. 60)?

13. How does a person know whether or not he has the gift of singleness? What is this gift to be exclusively used for (see p. 61)?

14. What passage of Scripture supports the fact that it's better to be single, in terms of service to Christ (see p. 61)?

15. Why aren't most people able to receive Jesus' teaching on marriage, divorce, and singleness (see pp. 61–62)?

16. What are the six reasons for marriage? Discuss each one (see pp. 62–64).

Pondering the Principles

1. If you're single, write down a list of the qualities you are looking for in a marriage partner. Now categorize these qualities into spiritual/physical and permanent/temporary. How many are physical and temporary? What category should the majority of these qualities be in? Prayerfully consider the qualities that you should be looking for in the person you will be spending the rest of your life with. Then, ask God to protect you from the deceitfulness of emotional, romantic feelings, and to give you wisdom and discernment when the need arises.

2. What effect does the easy access to divorce have upon problems in a marriage? Would a couple who do not believe in divorce deal with their problems differently? How and why? Are Christian marriages immune from problems? Why or why not? What advantages do Christian marriages have over non-Christian marriages? If you're married, take a moment right now to thank God for the partner He's given to you, and ask Him to continually remind you that you will be with this person for the rest of your life.

3. Look over the six reasons for marriage on pages 62–64 with your husband or wife. Now, on a scale of one to ten, evaluate your marriage in terms of fulfilling each one of these points. Spend some time in prayer together and thank God for His provision of marriage. Then ask God to help you fulfill His divine intention for your marriage.

5

Paul's Commentary on Divorce—
Part 1

Outline

Introduction

Review
 I. The Attack
 II. The Answer
 III. The Argument
 IV. The Affirmation
 V. The Appropriation

Lesson
 A. Morality in Corinth
 B. Marriages in the Roman Empire
   1. The confusion over definition
     a) *Contubernium*
     b) *Usus*
     c) *Coemptio in manum*
     d) *Confarreatio*
   2. The chaos causing divorce
     a) Homosexuality
     b) Polygamy
     c) Concubinage
     d) A women's liberation movement
 C. Messages to Paul

 I. Is Sex Unspiritual? (1 Cor. 7:1–7)
   A. The Question's Background
     1. Past sexual involvement
     2. Present spiritual intimidation
   B. The Question's Answer
     1. Celibacy is good
     2. Celibacy is tempting
     3. Celibacy is wrong for married people
       a) The obligation of marriage
       b) The only exception for abstinence
     4. Celibacy is a gift
       a) The awareness of celibacy
       b) The advantage of celibacy
       c) The appropriation of celibacy
         (1) A commended gift
         (2) A Corinthian problem

Review

I. THE ATTACK (v. 3; see pp. 7–10)

"The Pharisees also came unto him, testing him, and saying unto him, Is it lawful for a man to put away his wife for every cause?"

II. THE ANSWER (vv. 4–6; see pp. 10–15; 20–33)

"And he answered and said unto them, Have ye not read that he who made them at the beginning, made them male and female; and said, For this cause shall a man leave father and mother, and shall cleave to his wife, and they two shall be one flesh? Wherefore, they are no more two, but one flesh. What, therefore, God hath joined together, let not man put asunder."

III. THE ARGUMENT (v. 7; see pp. 39–43)

"They say unto him, Why did Moses then command to give a writing of divorcement, and to put her away?"

IV. THE AFFIRMATION (vv. 8–9; see pp. 43–49)

"He saith unto them, Moses, because of the hardness of your hearts, permitted you to put away your wives, but from the beginning it was not so. And I say unto you, Whosoever shall put away his wife, except it be for fornication, and shall marry another, committeth adultery; and whosoever marrieth her who is put away doth commit adultery."

V. THE APPROPRIATION (vv. 10–12; see pp. 54–64)

"His disciples say unto him, If the case of the man be so with his wife, it is not good to marry. But he said unto them, All men cannot receive this saying, except they to whom it is given. For there are some eunuchs, who were so born from their mother's womb; and there are some eunuchs, who were made eunuchs by men; and there are eunuchs, who have made themselves eunuchs for the kingdom of heaven's sake. He that is able to receive it, let him receive it."

Introduction

The Lord has given us very clear teaching on marriage and divorce. Marriage is honorable and for life—so stay married. Divorce is only permitted in the case of adultery. And even then, it should only occur when there is no possibility of reconciliation. When the disciples heard Jesus' teaching, they responded with the idea that it would be better to stay single. But Jesus said, "No, don't stay out of marriage because it takes a lifelong commitment. Get married for that very reason—unless, of course, you have a very clear reason not to. What reason? Unless you're single for the glory and advance of the kingdom." That's very clear teaching, isn't it?

You say, "Well, Jesus doesn't deal with a lot of the problems. For example, what does a person with a fouled-up background do when he comes to the Lord? Let's say he's living with someone who is not his wife, and he's been married five times before. Who is his wife?" Matthew 19 doesn't deal with any of that. Jesus is just establishing the divine ideal. It's not His intention to deal with the exceptions and all the other extraneous issues. Jesus, in affirming His messianic identity, lines up with the clear Word of the living God. And in so doing, He says to the people, "I speak for God." In fact, in Matthew 5:17 He essentially says, "I have come to fulfill the law, not to alter, eliminate, or destroy it." So, in Matthew 19 Jesus doesn't deal with all the exceptions, He simply affirms the divine ideal.

Also keep in mind that Jesus is talking to a Jewish group of people who have been living their entire life under the economy of Moses. In other words, they have been bound, to one degree or another, to their interpretation of the Mosaic law. So because they are in a Mosaic environment, Jesus simply states the intended ideal of God which was given to His special people, Israel.

You say, "Well, where does Scripture deal with all the problems? The ideal standards don't help me, because I've already violated them." Maybe you've had a divorce in your background, or you were living with someone when you became a Christian, or you've had several wives or husbands. You say, "Whose am I? What do I do? Can I ever remarry? What's going on?" Well, Jesus doesn't get into that, but fortunately Paul does—in 1 Corinthians 7. Jesus gave the divine ideal, but Paul had to handle the mess that was going on in the world and to make application of that divine ideal to the chaos of life.

Now keep this in mind: Paul ministered to a Gentile community that had not been raised to keep the law of Moses. So their life was a mess from beginning to end. There was much less chaos in the Jewish community because of the Mosaic legislation than there was in the Gentile one where there was no Mosaic legislation at all.

I believe that 1 Corinthians 7 is Paul's commentary on the teaching of Jesus about marriage and divorce. He interacts with the Lord's teaching in verse 10a: "And unto the married I command, yet not I, but the Lord." In other words, he reaches back, interfacing with what the Lord taught, and says, "Look, I'm going to tell you something about being married that isn't just from me; the Lord already said it." Then in verse 12a, he says, "But to the rest speak I, not the Lord." In other words, he says, "This is something new that the Lord didn't talk about. I'm no longer quoting the Lord." Now, he's not disclaiming inspiration; he's putting himself on an equal plane with the Lord Himself. He is saying, "The Lord didn't say this, but I'm saying it," which shows that what he's saying is just as important as if the Lord had said it!

The Problem with Red-Letter Bibles

You say, "Is what Paul said equally as important as what the Lord said?" Yes, it is! Why? Because both what the Lord said and what Paul said came from God. There are no degrees of inspiration. This is why I've always had a problem with the idea of red-letter Bibles. The red letters are *not* more important than the other letters! It's all right if you have a red-letter Bible, as long as you realize that the verses in red are not more important than any other verses.

At the end of 1 Corinthians 7, Paul further substantiates that what he says is on an equal plane with the sayings of the Lord. In verse 40b, he says, "I have the Spirit of God," as if to say, "I'm not just giving you my opinions" —even though verse 25a says, "Now concerning virgins, I have no commandment of the Lord; yet I give my judgment."

Paul, then, intersects with what the Lord taught—carrying it a bit further to cover the problems, issues, and struggles that the Corinthians were facing.

Lesson

Now, let me give you a little background of the situation in Corinth.

A. Morality in Corinth

The verb "to Corinthianize," in the Greek language, meant "to commit sexual sin." That just gives you a little idea of what Corinth was like. It was a rotten, wretched, sinful, vile place. So when someone wanted to refer to a person who was lecherous, evil, vile, lewd, lascivious, and adulterous, he would call that person a Corinthian. The people of Corinth were involved in worshiping all kinds of deities. When I visited the ruins of Corinth I saw gross replicas of human organs hanging all over the place. It was definitely a city characterized by the deviate worship of a pagan society.

A little church was born in that immoral, vile, wicked city by the wonderful ministry of the Spirit of God through the apostle Paul. And people were coming to Christ. However, these people didn't have a circumscribed, conformed background of what was moral and ethical—they came to Christ in an absolutely chaotic marital status.

B. Marriages in the Roman Empire

Much of the population of that part of the Roman world was slaves. Many of these slaves became Christians. In fact, some people believe that the majority of the early church was slaves. In a strict sense, marriage didn't even exist for slaves, because they were treated like animals. A farmer doesn't marry his cows or horses, he mates them. So, they didn't *marry* slaves, they *mated* them.

1. The confusion over definition

There were basically four different kinds of "marriages" in the Roman Empire.

a) *Contubernium*

This basically refers to a tent companionship. The slave owner would look over his slaves and mate them according to certain traits to produce the desired characteristics. There were never any ceremonies. They just entered into a live-in relationship similar to the live-in relationships of our contemporary society.

Let's say that a slave who has had different masters and different *contubernium* relationships suddenly becomes a Christian. Once he heard somebody stand up and teach what the Lord said about marriage (one man-one woman for life), he

69

would look at himself and think about all the women he may have had, all the children he might have spawned, and the woman he's currently living with. Then he would probably ask, "Now what do I do? Who is my wife?" It was a very real issue.

b) *Usus*

When we move one step beyond the slaves, we come to the marriage of the common people in the Roman culture. They were married under a custom called *usus*. Today we would call it common-law marriage. It basically stated that if you lived with someone for a year, you were considered to be legally married. So people tended to not get married at all. They would just experiment with different partners until they found one they liked. Then they would just stay with that particular partner for a year to make it legal. In America common-law marriage takes seven years, but I don't think anyone cares anymore.

What would happen if when you became a Christian, you were living with a woman whom you had been living with for three years, without ever marrying her? Is she your wife or isn't she? And what if you had had three other common-law wives before that, or one in this town and three in another town? It's very much like a missionary who goes to a foreign country, translates the Bible, and wins a tribe of people to Christ—only to find out, in the process, that they all have eight or ten wives. That's the kind of situation that Paul was dealing with in Corinth.

c) *Coemptio in manum*

A third kind of marriage in the inconsistent marital approaches of the Romans was called *coemptio in manum*. This was the old tradition of marriage by sale, where the man would buy the woman from her father. In other words, if you had a lousy business, but you also had a beautiful daughter, you could sell your daughter and bail out your business. This practice of selling off one's daughter into marriage was very common.

d) *Confarreatio*

The noble families of the Roman Empire had a sophisticated, fancy kind of marriage ceremony called *confarreatio*. It involved exchanging rings and placing them on the third finger of the left hand. This custom came from one of the Roman sages, who taught that there is a nerve running from that finger to the heart. They also had a cake, wore veils, had music, held right hands, and had wreaths. All of these traditions filtered down through the Roman Catholic marital system into Protestantism. We still have obvious remnants of it today, don't we?

Of all these strange marital situations, only the fourth one would really constitute a marriage as we understand it today—with the verbal commitment before people, the written covenant, and so forth. So the questions that came to Paul through the Corinthians were, "What in the world do we do with this hodgepodge of people coming to Christ? Who do they belong to? Do they have a right to remarry if they're now single? Should they stay living with the one they're living with in a *contubernium* relationship? What do we do with this mishmash of marriages?" and so on.

2. The chaos causing divorce

To add to the Corinthian problem, divorce was rampant. William Barclay notes that in one of the historical documents, a lady who was getting married for the twenty-seventh time was going to be the twenty-sixth wife of her husband-to-be. That will give you a little idea of how high the divorce rate was in those times. "Why was it so high?" you ask. Many factors contributed to the high divorce rate. Among them were:

a) Homosexuality

b) Polygamy

c) Concubinage

One of the Roman writers by the name of Seneca said that wives were for housekeeping and raising children and concubines were for physical pleasure.

d) A women's liberation movement

Jérôme Carcopino, in his book *Daily Life in Ancient Rome,* writes, "Some were not content to live their lives by their husband's side, but carried on another life without him" (p. 90). Quoting Juvenal, he says, "What modesty can you expect in a woman who wears a helmet, abjures her own sex, and delights in feats of strength?" (p. 92). Juvenal is also quoted as saying that women joined men's hunting parties, and "with spear in hand and breasts exposed, take to pig-sticking" (p. 92). Now that's not my kind of woman! Juvenal also said, "Thus does she lord it over her husband. But before long she vacates her kingdom; she flits from one home to another wearing out her bridal veil" (p. 99).

So what do you do with all these people who come to Christ out of this chaos? It's like trying to unscramble an omelet! The Corinthians didn't know what to do, so they wrote a letter to Paul—a letter that is alluded to in 1 Corinthians 7.

C. Messages to Paul

First Corinthians 7:1 starts out, "Now concerning the things about which ye wrote unto me." That sets up the entire chapter. He's going to answer their questions, but you know what he does? He doesn't tell us the questions; he gives us the answers. So, to understand 1 Corinthians 7, we have to figure out the original questions asked by the Corinthians from the answers given by Paul. I'll tell you one thing, though. Paul covers every category you can think of. For example, he covers single people, married people, people married to believers, and people married to unbelievers. He discusses whether or not a person who is divorced and now single has the right to marry, whether or not a father with virgin daughters should give them in marriage, and whether or not a person whose husband or wife has died should remarry. He covers all these questions in this chapter.

I. IS SEX UNSPIRITUAL? (1 Cor. 7:1–7)

A. The Question's Background

1. Past sexual involvement

Can you imagine coming out of this terrible background of sexual chaos? In your worship of pagan gods you may have been involved with the prostitute temple priestesses. You might have been involved in multiple marriage and divorce or sexual relationships without any marriage at all. And you would have been part of a society that advocated homosexuality, adultery, polygamy, and so on. You name it, they were promoting it. Those people who came to Jesus Christ out of that background still had their minds filled with all of that garbage.

2. Present spiritual intimidation

Apparently, someone had gotten up in the Corinthian church and given a lesson on the fact that all sex is unspiritual. And with their kind of background, you can understand why someone might do that. Even married people might have had problems enjoying the marital relationship honored by God, because of all the garbage and filth of their past. Somebody probably came along and said, "All sex is evil. It's all bad. It's not spiritual. If you want to be spiritual, abstain."

So the Corinthians wrote Paul and asked a legitimate question, "Is sex really unspiritual?"

B. The Question's Answer

1. Celibacy is good (v. 1b)

"It is good for a man not to touch a woman."

The phrase "touch a woman" is the key to this verse. It is a euphemism for sexual intercourse, as seen in such passages as Genesis 20:6 and Proverbs 6:29. So Paul says, "It's good not to have a sexual relationship with someone." It's good (Gk., *kalos*) —which means it's OK, beneficial, honorable, all right. In other words, Paul is saying that it's okay to be celibate. It's not wrong not to marry. Celibacy is good, honorable, and excellent.

2. Celibacy is tempting (v. 2)

"Nevertheless, to avoid fornication, let every man have his own wife, and let every woman have her own husband."

"Celibacy may be a good thing," says Paul, "but for most folks it's pretty tempting. So if your celibacy is going to cause you to sin sexually, either physically or in your mind, then you ought to have your own partner." That's Paul's point. It's OK to be a celibate, but not if it's going to cause you to sin. So the idea of the "swinging single life" is not OK—but it is OK to totally abstain from sexual relationships. We saw that in Matthew 19:12, didn't we? Maybe you have a congenital reason for your single-ness, or maybe you had an accident which prohibits you from having a sexual relationship, or maybe you have decided to be single for the sake of the kingdom of heaven (see pp. 60–61). For any of those reasons, it's OK to be single. In fact, as we shall see later, it's even better than just OK, it may be the best—for some.

So Paul says, "In answer to your question, celibacy is good." Now if Paul had said, "Oh no, you should never be celibate," then all the people who wanted to be celibate their entire life for the sake of the kingdom would feel disobedient. So he says, "It's good, but if it's going to cause you temptation, and you're going to get into sexual sin, then you ought to have your own wife or husband." By the way, the word "own" in verse 2 shows monogamy, doesn't it? You are to have your *own* wife or husband—and that's it.

The style of life among the Corinthians made it harder to be single than to be married. The people who wanted to live a life of celibacy for the cause of the Lord were living in the midst of a sex-mad society, where it would be nothing but a constant temptation.

Celibacy is good, but marriage is more common. Celibacy is also tempting, so don't stay single if it's going to cause you to commit sexual sin.

3. Celibacy is wrong for married people (vv. 3–5)

    a) The obligation of marriage (vv. 3–4)

        "Let the husband render unto the wife her due [or 'the debt']; and likewise also, the wife unto the husband. The wife hath not power of her own body, but the husband; and likewise also the husband hath not power of his own body, but the wife."

        There's no place for celibacy in marriage. The word "due" is literally "the debt" and means "the obligation." In other words, when you get married, you become obligated to meet the physical needs of your partner. And according to verse 4, you also give up the right to your own body—it belongs to your partner.

        Verse 3, which is in the present imperative in the Greek, literally reads, "Let the husband continually keep on render-ing to his wife the debt, and likewise also let the wife keep on rendering the debt she owes her husband." In other words, the sexual relationship in marriage is to be a continual giving—a continual submission to one another. And believe me, when this does not happen, it will destroy a marriage. There must be a growing intimacy of two lives, blended together in all dimensions, into an unbreakable bond of love.

Marriage is no place for celibacy. You're not more spiritual if you abstain from sex in your marriage. I want to make a point of this, because there is teaching going around today that says you can gain a greater amount of spirituality by abstaining from physical relationships in marriage. Don't believe it!

b) The only exception for abstinence (v. 5)

"Defraud ye not one the other, except it be with consent for a time, that ye may give yourselves to fasting and prayer; and come together again, that Satan tempt you not for your incontinency."

If you try to abstain from each other, for some spiritual purpose other than for a brief time of prayer and fasting that you have mutually consented to, you won't accomplish a spiritual purpose—you'll accomplish an evil one. Why? Because you'll put the person in the place of being open to the solicitation of temptation by Satan himself.

Sexual Abstinence in Marriage: Design or Delusion?

Recently a teaching has been going around that says we should abstain fourteen days a month for spiritual purposes. Some marriages would be literally destroyed by that because people's needs are different. The only thing the New Testament says is that we are to give ourselves totally to our partner. Abstaining from the sexual relationship of marriage for fourteen days a month as a means to spiritual development is, in fact, a means to satanic temptation—in most cases.

You say, "Where are they getting the basis for this teaching?" Well, they're going back to Leviticus 15 where Moses is describing the ceremonial law. In verse 19 it says that when a woman goes through her monthly menstrual cycle, she is ceremonially unclean for a period of seven days. Now that doesn't mean she's immoral! It's not immoral to have a normal, God-given cycle. It's not an issue of morality or ethics or spirituality. It is simply a ceremonial uncleanness. All the ceremonies were signs and symbols—not realities! So for that seven-day period, she was ceremonially unclean.

Now, according to verses 28–30, at the end of seven days, she needed another seven days of purification where she would go through certain washings and ceremonies. Then, on the fifteenth day, she would take two turtledoves or two pigeons and give them to the priest—who would sacrifice them on the altar. At that point, she could enter in to worship God.

The whole point of this ritual was to show that they were not to approach God while they were unclean. God was not really driving at physical uncleanness, He was driving at the necessity of a clean heart—just like a circumcision. Every time a Jewish baby was circumcised, the Jews had to think back through the fact that as the foreskin was being cut away, the heart needed to be circumcised as well, by the cutting away of all evil. So a woman wasn't morally unclean or spiritually unfit for fourteen days a month, it was simply an outward demonstration of the inward reality that a person can't approach God unless the heart is clean. The Old Testament sacrifices accomplished the same purpose. Were they able to take away sin? No, and neither was any kind of washing or ceremonial cleansing. They were simply symbolic.

When Christ came, He finished the work on the cross, gave us a new heart, and cleaned us from the inside out. Now we have boldness to enter into the Holy of Holies (Heb. 10:19), so we cannot advocate that we need the same fourteen days of purification. However, those who do advocate this say, "Well, in Leviticus it says that if a husband has a relationship with his wife during that period, he becomes ceremonially unclean, and has to go through a certain cleansing process too." Now, that doesn't mean it's wrong for him to have a sexual relationship with his wife, or that it's immoral or unspiritual. All it means is this: If he does have a relationship with his wife during this period of time, he will have to go through a certain ceremony which will act as a reminder to him as well.

By the way, I'm quite confident that the Jews didn't see this as fourteen days a month of abstinence. So it was probably very common for them to be going through this cleansing. In fact, I believe that God gave this particular cleansing connected with this particular act between husband and wife because its common occurrence would cause them to be commonly reminded of the fact that God must be approached by those who have clean hands and a pure heart. It was only symbolic!

My question to the person who advocates fourteen days a month of sexual abstinence in marriage is this: When the fourteen days are up, are you going to have the woman find two turtledoves, one priest, and a temple somewhere to make a sacrifice? Because either the cross eliminates all of it or none of it! You see, the New Testament doesn't say anything like that. What it does say, however, is this: "Keep on giving yourself to each other, and don't stop doing that unless, by mutual consent, you go to prayer over some issue that is so heartrending that sex becomes a nonconcern to you. But other than that, continually be giving yourselves to each other. Otherwise, you're not going to get more spiritual, you're going to give Satan an opportunity to tempt you and to foul up your marriage." The Old Covenant has ended, folks. There were a lot of ceremonies in the Old Covenant that we just don't maintain today.

And if you're going to pick up that one, then you're going to have to pick up a lot of other baggage with it—like a bunch of rams and lambs. Furthermore, finding the high priest and the Temple isn't going to be easy, since the last one we know of was destroyed in 70 A.D.

When you start trying to take Old Covenant ceremonial symbols and drag them into the New, you're doing exactly what the apostle Paul said not to do in Colossians 2. He referred to all the ceremonies as merely a shadow, and Christ as the reality. So, since the reality has come, we're not to let anyone bind us to the shadows.

First Corinthians 7:1–7 is answering the question: Is sex unspiritual? And the answer is: Of course not. God invented and designed it and intended for it to be the fulfillment of man. In fact, there is no fulfillment in life that can even match it. It's a marvelous thing. We're not called upon in the Bible to abstain from it; we're called upon in the Bible to enjoy it to its fullest, so that we can build a tremendous and profound intimacy with our partner that will last a lifetime. To abstain is to give Satan an advantage over us.

4. Celibacy is a gift (vv. 6–7)

   a) The awareness of celibacy (v. 6)

   "But I speak this by permission [or 'because of my awareness'], and not by commandment."

   In other words, Paul says, "I'm not commanding people to get married. I'm just aware of the fact that most people need that. What I know about life tells me that it's okay to be celibate; but to avoid fornication, you ought to have your own husband or your own wife. And once you get married, don't let anyone tell you that it's more spiritual to abstain." Hebrews 13:4*a* says, "Marriage is honorable in all, and the bed undefiled." It's a holy and sacred place.

   b) The advantage of celibacy (v. 7*a*)

   "For I would that all men were even as I myself."

   There's a sense in which Paul wishes that everybody could be single and celibate. He was celibate. Now, he may have been married at one time, since some say that all members of the Sanhedrin had to be married. If he was married, his wife was now dead and definitely a forgotten woman, in terms of biblical revelation. But now he's single and saying, "I would that all men were even as I myself."

   Paul makes this statement because he realizes that in singleness there is great freedom—great liberty. For example, in verses 29–30*a* of this chapter Paul says, "But this I say, brethren. The time is short; it remaineth that both they that have wives be as though they had none; and they that weep, as though they wept not; and they that rejoice, as though they rejoiced not.'' In other words, we have to turn away from the things of this life; and because the time is short, we're to focus on divine things.

Then in verse 32a, Paul says, ''But I would have you without care [or 'anxiety']. In other words, ''I wish you were carefree like I am.'' You know, there's a certain carefree reality about being single. You don't have to care for a wife and children and all the things that come along with it. It's an anxiety-free lifestyle, in that sense. You say, ''I'm single, but I'm not anxiety free!'' Well, that may be a good indication that you ought to be looking toward marriage. If you're single and struggling with your physical desires then maybe you'd better lower your standard from waiting for the local Adonis to show up and take some man that has a heart for God. And all you men, find a woman that has a heart for God too. Instead of fighting through the jungle of your own temptation, allow God to fulfill and enrich your life with someone who has the same values that you do in Jesus Christ. Quit restricting yourself to some silly standards that the world has established.

c) The appropriation of celibacy (v. 7b)

''But every man hath his proper gift of God, one after this manner, and another after that.''

Paul says, ''Look, I'm not going to argue with God's gift. I don't want people who need to be married trying to live a celibate life—at least not traveling in my missionary team! That doesn't help! I just know that God wants some people single and some married. If God wants you married, then get married. You ought to have your own wife or husband.''

(1) A commended gift

I believe that verse 7 proves that singleness is a gift of God. God suits some people for marriage, and God suits some people for singleness. And you know you've been gifted for singleness if you feel you can handle it without it posing a temptation to you and if your desire is to give your concentrated heart attention to the advance of the kingdom.

Go back to the middle of verse 32: ''He that is unmarried careth for the things that belong to the Lord, how he may please the Lord; but he that is married careth for the things that are of the world, how he may please his wife. There is difference also between a wife and a virgin. The unmarried woman careth for the things of the Lord, that she may be holy both in body and in spirit; but she that is married careth for the things of the world, how she may please her husband'' (vv. 32b–34). In other words, you get some baggage when you get married. You say, ''I

77

need that!'' Well, if you do, you should get married. But if you can stay single without it posing a temptation to you, than you can have a marvelous, thrilling, God-given opportunity to give your life to the advancement of the kingdom of God.

Don't stay single because you just don't want to make a commitment, and then end up trying to fight temptation for the rest of your life. Only make a commitment to stay single if you believe that God has gifted you in that area, if you don't need the physical fulfillment that marriage brings, and if you can see yourself as totally and utterly devoted to Jesus Christ. It's a marvelous gift that God gives to some.

(2) A Corinthian problem

Apparently, whoever gave the message in the Corinthian church saying that it was more spiritual to remain single got so many people stirred up that some of the fathers were reluctant to give their daughters in marriage. They may have even been trying to hold their daughters back from getting married, which would have been a terrible frustration to the daughters. I think that is what Paul is referring to in verse 36 when he says, "But if any man think that he behaveth unseemly toward his virgin [or 'daughter'], if she pass the flower of her age, and need so require, let him do what he will, he sinneth not; let them marry."

Here's a man with a beautiful daughter who wants to get married, and he says, "No, you're for the Lord. I'm going to keep you single for the Lord." And I can just hear her saying, "But I don't want to be single for the Lord, Daddy. I want Albert!" The father is trying to force some spiritual standard on her, when all she wants is a husband and kids. So Paul says, "Look, let them marry."

Somebody had really given them a line on abstinence that was out of line with God's truth. It's great to be married, if that's what God has called you to. I wouldn't trade all the joys of having a loving wife and blessed children and family. That's life to me. But I also know there are some people who are single for the glory of God, who wouldn't trade either. Paul was one of them!

Was Peter Married?

In 1 Corinthians 9:5 Paul affirms his rights as an apostle and says, "Have we no right to lead about a sister, a wife, as well as other apostles, and as the brethren of the Lord, and Cephas?" In other words, he says, "Look, if I wanted to, I have a right to get married." It isn't more spiritual to be single. It isn't more spiritual at all. Paul says, "I could be married like Peter."

Did you know that Peter was married? We see his wife's mother in the gospels (Matt. 8:14; Mark 1:30; Luke 4:38), and here in 1 Corinthians we're reminded that he has a wife. Peter was married and Paul was not; nevertheless, both were great apostles. God used Peter in a mighty way, although he apparently didn't travel as much as Paul—possibly because of the encumbering of his family. Paul had the unique freedom of singleness, although he did have the right to lead about a sister as a wife—just like everybody else. Marriage is a wonderful, honorable, and God-blessed provision; and singleness is only for the glory of God, not because people are unwilling to make a commitment, or because they've set some worldly standard for whom they will marry and nobody comes up to that standard.

By the way, there's a couple of footnotes in 1 Corinthians 9:5 that I can't resist. Paul tells us two things about a wife—she needs to be led, and she ought to be a sister. This is a wonderful affirmation of what the Bible says about male responsibility, to be the head and to lead his wife. Now it's not saying to put a ring in her nose and drag her around. I believe Paul is saying that the husband is to give guidance and direction to his wife. That's God's intention. And not only is she to be one who will follow and be led, she is to be a sister in Christ.

The question, then, in the first seven verses of 1 Corinthians 7 is this: Is sex unspiritual? The answer is: No, sex is not unspiritual. It's OK if you're a virgin until you die. It's an honorable calling if God gifts you for that life-style and sets you apart to do the work of the kingdom. If you've been married in the past and now you're single again—either through death or divorce—your first thought ought to be, "Maybe God wants me to stay single now." That's honorable, that's OK, that's good. From here on out, you could be celibate and glorify God. However, marriage also glorifies God. It just depends on what your gift is.

So we've seen the first question of 1 Corinthians 7, Is sex unspiritual? In our next lesson we'll look at the rest of chapter 7 and six more questions on this extremely vital subject of marriage and divorce.

Focusing on the Facts

1. In Matthew 19, does Jesus deal with all the problems of divorce and remarriage? Why or why not? Where are these problems dealt with in Scripture and by whom (see pp. 67–68)?

2. What was the main difference between the group of people that Jesus was addressing in Matthew 19 and the group of people that Paul was addressing in 1 Corinthians 7? Why would this make a difference in the content of their teaching on divorce and remarriage (see p. 68)?

3. What gives the indication that 1 Corinthians 7 is Paul's commentary on Jesus' teaching on divorce (see p. 68)?

4. Are the teachings of Jesus more important than the teachings of Paul or any other New Testament writer? Why or why not (see p. 68)?

5. When Paul says, in 1 Corinthians 7:12, that he is speaking and not the Lord, is he saying that he's just giving his opinion and nothing more? Explain (see p. 68).

6. In terms of morality, what was the city of Corinth like? How does our modern society compare with Corinth (see p. 69)?

7. What were the four different kinds of "marriages" in the Roman Empire at the time of Paul? Define each one (see pp. 69–70).

8. What were some of the factors that contributed to the high divorce rate in the Roman Empire (see p. 71)?

9. According to 1 Corinthians 7:1a, what was the overall reason Paul wrote this chapter? How can we determine the questions the Corinthians asked Paul (see pp. 71–72)?

10. What specific question does Paul answer in verses 1–7? Why was this even an issue to the Corinthians (see p. 72)?

11. What does the phrase "touch a woman" mean in 1 Corinthians 7:1? What does this verse say about celibacy (see pp. 72–73)?

12. According to verse 2, what is an important reason to get married (see pp. 72–73)?

13. Why would it have been especially difficult for the Christians in Corinth to live a life of celibacy (see p. 73)?

14. Verse 3 says that the husband is to "render unto the wife her due." What does this mean (see pp. 73–74)?

15. According to verses 3–4, who is to submit in the sexual relationship of marriage? What will happen in a marriage if this is not carried out (see pp. 73–74)?

16. What is the only exception for sexual abstinence in marriage? What is the danger in abstaining for extended periods of time (see p. 74)?

17. In the Old Testament, why was a woman considered unclean for fourteen days a month? What was the intention behind this ceremonial law? Why can't we legitimately use this to advocate fourteen days of sexual abstinence in marriage for spiritual purposes (see pp. 74–75)?

18. According to verse 6, what wasn't Paul commanding the Corinthians to do? Why (see p. 76)?

19. In terms of service to the Lord, would Paul say it's better to be married or single? Why? Use Scripture to support your answer (see p. 76).

20. How would you be able to determine if you had the gift of celibacy (see p. 77)?

21. How do we know that Peter was married? Was Paul more spiritual because he was a celibate? Explain (see pp. 78–79).

22. In 1 Corinthians 9:5, Paul tells us two things about a wife. What are they (see p. 79)?

23. Summarize Paul's answer to the question: Is sex unspiritual (see p. 79)?

Pondering the Principles

1. As we were going through Jesus' teaching on divorce in Matthew 19, did you ever think, "These ideals are great, but what do I do if I've already violated them? What do I do if I'm divorced, or divorced and remarried?" If you have questions regarding your marital status, read through the entire chapter of 1 Corinthians 7 as a basis for what we are going to be studying in our remaining lessons. Then ask God, through His Word, to answer your specific question.

2. Have you ever met single Christians in their late twenties or thirties and thought, "I wonder what's wrong with them. I wonder why they're not married yet"? What's wrong with that kind of thinking? Have you ever considered the possibility that God has gifted them in a special way so that they could serve Him in a more unhindered and devoted way? Get to know these people and become involved in their lives. They need your fellowship, and you'll be blessed by theirs.

3. On a scale of one to ten, evaluate the sexual relationship in your marriage on the basis of 1 Corinthians 7:3–4. What does it mean that the husband and wife have the "power" of each other's body? Make a commitment to totally submit your body to your spouse. To do less is to violate God's Word!

4. Read 1 Corinthians 7:5 and answer the following questions: Should you ever abstain from sex in marriage without the approval of your spouse? To do so would be to do what to your partner? What is the only reason that abstinence is permitted in marriage? Should there be a specified period of time for this abstinence? Why? Consider the following: When you withhold sex from your partner without mutual consent, for an undetermined period of time, for any reason other than prayer, you put your partner in a place where Satan will tempt him or her toward lack of self-control and possibly adultery. Commit yourself to fulfill your obligation in marriage to meet the sexual needs of your partner.

6
Paul's Commentary on Divorce—Part 2

Outline

Introduction

Review
I. Is Sex Unspiritual?
  A. The Question's Background
  B. The Question's Answer

Lesson
II. Should Those That Are Formerly Married Remarry?
  A. The Question's Background
  B. The Question's Answer
    1. The participants of remarriage
      a) The categories of singleness
        (1) virgins
        (2) widows
        (3) unmarried
      b) The clarification of the term ''unmarried''
        (1) Demonstrated
          (a) Verse 32b
          (b) Verse 34a
          (c) Verse 8a
          (d) Verses 10b–11a
        (2) Defined
    2. The provision of remarriage
    3. The passion of remarriage
III. What Are the Alternatives for Those That Are Married
  A. The Question's Background
  B. The Question's Answer
    1. A Christian married to another Christian
      a) The command to stay married
      b) The check against further sin
    2. A Christian married to a non-Christian
      a) If the unbeliever wants to stay
        (1) Stay together
        (2) Sanctify the family
      b) If the unbeliever divorces
        (1) God's call to peace
        (2) God's caution against marital evangelism

Introduction

One of the areas in which the Bible gives very clear teaching is in the area of divorce and remarriage. We cannot alter that. We cannot change it to accommodate our "sophisticated day." We cannot go to the Bible with our contemporary ideas and change the Scripture or eliminate the principles that we feel are an intrusion on our life patterns. We must objectively and openly hear what the Bible says—and obey it.

Our Lord gave us a very clear statement in regard to divorce in Matthew 19:1–2. The Pharisees came to Jesus in verse 3 and said, "Is it lawful for a man to put away [divorce] his wife for every cause?" Jesus answered, in effect, and said, "No, you cannot get a divorce for every cause. There's only one cause in the law of God for God's people to divorce—hard-hearted adultery. And only then is the innocent partner free to remarry." Now that is a simple statement. I really don't think it's too confusing if you understand the Scripture. You can go to the Bible with your pre-conceptions and come up with a lot of ideas—and people have done that and confused the church in many ways—but it's very clear if you just take it from the text.

The problem with Matthew 19 is that it's too isolated. It doesn't tell us about all the exceptions or answer all of our myriad questions. It just lays down one principle. So in order to broaden our understanding, we must go elsewhere in the New Testament. I want to take you now to 1 Corinthians chapter 7, because I believe this chapter is Paul's commentary on the divine principle, on the divine law, on the teaching of our Lord.

Keep in mind that Paul was dealing in a society much like ours. He was not talking to a Jewish society like our Lord was—a society that had been reared on Mosaic law, where people were trying to conform to the divine standard. He was talking to an utterly pagan society who had no relationship to the law of God, whose background was literally jammed full of incongruities in terms of God's law, and who was in and out of marriages and relationships *ad infinitum, ad nauseam.* These people were now coming to Christ and asking very basic questions, "What is my status?" "Where do I stand?" and so forth.

The Corinthians wrote a letter to Paul. First Corinthians 7:1*a* tells us about it; "Now concerning the things about which ye wrote unto me." They wrote him a letter to find out about these issues and to have him tell them just what the situation was. So they asked him a series of questions that he answers in chapter 7. In our last lesson, we looked at the first question.

Review

I. IS SEX UNSPIRITUAL? (vv. 1–7; see pp. 72–79)

A. The Question's Background

The first question they asked him was, "Is sex unspiritual?" Naturally, if you had come out of the kind of life-style that they had, and lived in the midst of that kind of filth, lewdness, and pornographic approach to life, you might just say, "Now that I'm a Christian, I'm just going to forget all that sexual stuff." And even though you would want to clean up your life and do it right, your mind would be so flooded with the garbage of the past, that it would be really hard to have a pure relationship in your mind. It would take a long time to divorce yourself from all the garbage that cluttered up your thinking. And so, some people were saying, "We just need to stop having sexual relationships altogether." Also, to add to the problem, somebody was probably teaching the Corinthians that all sex was unspiritual anyway. And since it was all evil and sinful, Christians ought to eliminate it altogether.

B. The Question's Answer

Paul answers the question in verses 1–7 by saying, "No, sex is not unspiritual. It's OK not to engage in that if God has called you to a life of singleness and has given you the gift to deal with that. But it's also OK to be married. However, if you are married, it's not OK to be celibate." So sex is not unspiritual. Sex is very spiritual. It's created by God as the most obvious affirmation of the one-flesh truth. Keep in mind, though, that if you are single, it's not for freedom's sake, or for promiscuity's sake, or for lack of commitment's sake; it's for the service of the kingdom.

Let's continue on and look at the second question Paul answers.

Lesson

II. SHOULD THOSE THAT ARE FORMERLY MARRIED REMARRY? (vv. 8–9)

A. The Question's Background

This is really a key question in the Corinthian church. Single people came to Christ who used to be married. Now that they have become Christians, do they have the right to marry again? Or, if they made a mistake in the past prior to salvation, are they stuck with the consequences for the rest of their lives? That's the issue. And I believe what the apostle Paul says in verses 8–9 refers to those people who are now single but before conversion were married. It's the only interpretation that makes sense out of this passage. I'll show you why as we look at it.

Now this is also a real issue for all of us to understand today. Many people in our churches, who have come to Christ as formerly-married singles, want to know whether they have a right to marry. I believe these verses speak to this issue.

B. The Question's Answer

1. The participants of remarriage (v. 8a)

"I say therefore, to the unmarried and widows."

a) The categories of singleness

Now, note the two categories—the unmarried and the widows. There is one other major category in this chapter, and it is in verse 25, "Now concerning virgins." This chapter deals with the unmarried, the widowed, and virgins. Those are the three classes of single people. Now, let's understand what those classes are.

(1) Virgins

Virgins (Gk., *parthenoi*) are single people who have never been married.

(2) Widows

Widows (Gk., *cherais*) are single people who formerly were married but were released from that marriage by death.

(3) Unmarried

Now that leaves us with the "unmarried"—a key term in this chapter. But who are the unmarried? I believe this is a key interpretive word if we're going to understand this chapter, and I don't think that anything I've ever read

85

really deals with this term. So I hope I can make some contribution to that in this message.

b) The clarification of the term "unmarried"

  (1) Demonstrated

The term "unmarried" is used only four times in the entire New Testament. And all four occurrences are here in 1 Corinthians 7. So, this is where we have to get our understanding of it.

    (*a*) Verse 32*b*—"He that is unmarried careth for the things that belong to the Lord, how he may please the Lord." It's used very generally there. It's just a general statement about one that is unmarried (v. 32), as opposed to one that is married (v. 33).

    (*b*) Verse 34*a*—Here Paul uses the term in a more technical way. He says, "And the woman who is unmarried, and the virgin, is concerned about the things of the Lord, that she may be holy both in body and spirit" (NASB). Here he uses "unmarried" along with "virgin." So he must be talking about two different categories. Whoever the unmarried are, they aren't virgins. So now we have two groups, and the unmarried category is narrowing down a little bit.

    (*c*) Verse 8*a*—"I say, therefore, to the unmarried and widows." Now watch carefully. From verse 34 we learn that the unmarried aren't virgins, right? And from verse 8 we learn that the unmarried aren't widows either. You say, "If the term 'unmarried' isn't referring to the virgins, and it isn't referring to the widows, who is it referring to?"

    (*d*) Verses 10*b*–11*a*—"Let not the wife [divorce] her husband; but and if she [divorces], let her remain unmarried." Now you have the specific meaning of the word "unmarried." It refers to people who were divorced. That's what it says!

  (2) Defined

In verse 8 there are two categories of single people—the unmarried and the widows. Both are formerly married people. The widows were formerly married until death, and the unmarried were formerly married until divorce. When you go to verse 34, you have the virgin and the unmarried. That speaks of single people—some who have never been married and some who have been formerly married.

So the only way to really understand the word here is to understand it as referring to formerly married people. It is not referring to virgins or widows, because it's used with both those words. When it is used alone in verse 11 it is referring to someone who has divorced. The word "unmarried," then, refers to people who were formerly married but are not widows—people who are now single but are not virgins.

I also believe that Paul is talking to people who were divorced before coming to Christ. They came to Christ and then began to ask the question, "Now do I have a right to marry?" For example, let's say I had married twice and divorced twice before I became a Christian. I could have been guilty of adultery or divorced for many other reasons. In fact, I didn't even think of God's law, it was just my former life-style. Now I'm single. Do I have a right to remarry? Or let's say I'm widowed. Do I have a right to remarry? What does Paul say?

2. The provision of remarriage (vv. 8b–9a)

"It is good for them if they abide even as I. But if they [both groups] cannot have self-control, let them marry."

Now this is God's provision for those people now single, who were formerly married prior to their conversion. That's the only interpretation that makes any sense out of this passage. Why? Because that's the question they're asking. You go over to verses 17–24, and all through that whole passage the implication is: "Now that I've become a Christian, what do I change?" Basically, Paul's answer to that is, "Don't change anything. Stay in the state you are in. Stay single if you can. If you can't, get married." Why?

3. The passion of remarriage (v. 9b)

"For it is better to marry than to burn [with lust or passion]."

It is better to get married than to spend your whole life fighting off the threat of fornication or adultery because you can't control your passion. God did not create you with that desire and that drive in order to live an entire life of absolute frustration. If you can stay single, stay single. It's a gift of God. If you can't, even though you were formerly married, you are given not only the right but the instruction to get married. Why? Because it's better to marry than to go through life burning with lust or passion.

And so, when a person becomes a Christian, I think there's a dawning of a new day. I think there's something brand new that happens. And the grace of Jesus Christ that saves the soul also saves the body from a lifetime of utter frustration and anxiety. There's no point in that, because "if any man be in Christ, he is a new creation" (2 Cor. 5:17a). Everything starts all over again. God obviously permits the widows to remarry. And here, I believe, He permits the formerly married to marry as well. So whether single by death or single by divorce, there is that right and that privilege.

It's better to marry than to burn. That's why Paul in 1 Timothy 5, when he talks about the young widows, says, "Don't let them assign themselves to a life of service to Christ. Of course if they're gifted for it, fine. But don't let them hurry to do that because the time's going to come when they will grow wanton against Christ." In other words, they're going to be sorry that they took that vow, because they're going to want a husband—and then they're going to have lust problems. "So," says Paul, "it's better for the widows— the young ones—to marry." First Timothy 5 affirms the same thing. It is better to marry than to burn.

So don't restrain someone who comes to Jesus Christ by saying, "Well, you were responsible to live the law of God all your life long—even before you were saved, knew the law of God, or even cared about the law of God. And if you ever made a mistake in the life that you lived prior to Christ, you're stuck." I don't see that as the intention of this passage or of the heart of God.

Now that ought to be liberating for some folks. God is a God of grace and a God of liberation. But let me just give you a little bit of advice. Think through very carefully if, in fact, you should not stay single—because that seems to be Paul's priority. But if you do remarry, would you pick up the note at the end of verse 39 and remember that you are to marry "only in the Lord"? You say, "What does that mean?" Only a Christian and only in the will of God. You could marry a Christian but the wrong Christian. So not only are you to marry a Christian, you're to marry the right one. And that's only determined as you seek to know His will and as He leads and guides you.

What to do while you're waiting for marriage

It is God's intention that you remarry if, in fact, you're made for marriage. That's the grace of God. Now if there's a gap between your right to remarry and its fulfillment, the question always comes up, "How am I going to handle that? How am I going to handle the anxiety and the pressure that arises when you know you need to marry, you want to marry, and you're made to marry, but you can't get it fulfilled? And how do you deal with the problem of burning with desire?" Well, let me give you some practical suggestions:

1. Channel your energy through physical work and spiritual ministry. Idle moments don't help—at all.

2. Stay close to and accountable to a Christian friend. Don't live alone, travel alone, go places alone, or do things alone where you will be vulnerable. Also, stick close to someone whom you can be accountable to—someone who is mature and who understands your needs.

3. Pray for purity and stay in the Word.

4. Don't seek only to get married. Don't take just any plane that's leaving the airport—figure out where you want to go before you

88

get on. Seek to honor Christ in your life and in relationships of friendship, and let God bring about a marriage.

5. Avoid sex-mad, adulterous, worldly temptations. Be careful what you let into your senses—what you see, what you hear, and where you go—because whatever you allow in is going to have an impact on you.

6. Count on divine enabling to live for now without fulfillment. Count on God to give you the strength.

7. Avoid all potentially dangerous situations. Stay away from them, because even though you may feel you're innocent, you may not be able to control somebody else.

8. Praise God in the midst of it and be content. Praise has a very wholesome effect.

Now if you're the kind of person that follows these principles, people will be beating a path to your door to marry you. Why? Because those are the kind of people other folks are looking for. And when the right one comes along let me give you a little advice: Have a spiritual relationship and a short engagement.

Question number two: Should formerly married people remarry? The answer is—it's optional. If you can stay single, stay single. If you can't, then marry. It's OK, because it's better to marry than to burn.

There's a third implied question in the passage.

III. WHAT ARE THE ALTERNATIVES FOR THOSE THAT ARE MARRIED? (vv. 10–16)

A. The Question's Background

Do you know what was happening in Corinth? When people became Christians, they said, "Boy, I'm married to an unsaved partner. I think I should get rid of him/her. After all, my spouse doesn't even understand the things of the Lord." Not only that, I'm sure somebody was teaching, "You have to get rid of your unsaved partner because the devil is in your house corrupting your kids. You can't walk together unless you be agreed, and you can't have light with darkness. You have to get rid of that unsaved partner—Beelzebub." I can just hear somebody waxing eloquent on that kind of thing— really making it sound good. So the temptation would be to just get rid of the unsaved partner.

Now if both the husband and the wife became Christians after their marriage, one of them might say, "I want to be a spiritual Christian, but I'm not real happy with this union we made before we were saved. Now that we're Christians, we both have different approaches to life. We're not getting along, so let's just start all over again. Let's just dump each other and get another marriage going."

The question Paul has to answer is this, "What happens now that I've become a Christian? I'm still married, but do I have to stay married, or can I shed my partner? What are my rights and privileges in that regard?''

B. The Question's Answer

 1. A Christian married to another Christian (vv. 10–11)

   a) The command to stay married (vv. 10, 11*b*)

   "And unto the married I command, yet not I, but the Lord, Let not the wife [divorce] her husband . . . and let not the husband [divorce] his wife."

   Paul goes right back to Matthew 5 and 19, and right back to God's standard from the very beginning in Genesis 1:27 and 2:24, and says, "If you're married, stay married." And I believe he's referring here to two Christians, because in verse 12 he says, "But to the rest speak I, not the Lord," where he speaks of a Christian married to a non-Christian. So because he doesn't get to a mixed marriage until verse 12, he must be referring to two Christians. Paul's answer to two married people who come to the Lord is this, "Stay married, don't divorce!"

   b) The check against further sin (v. 11*a*)

   "But and if she [divorce], let her remain unmarried, or be reconciled to her husband."

   Do you know what? Paul knew that some people would disobey God and get a divorce. So he says, "If you're going to disobey God at point one, stop there, would you?" You can tell people what God wants, but they'll go and do what they want anyway. So he sets up another roadblock, and says, "If you break law one, please stop there. Don't go any further." Now, Paul is not saying that it's OK to get a divorce. He's simply saying that if you're going to be disobedient there, don't go any further. Because if you divorce, you only have two options: remain formerly married for the rest of your life, or be reconciled to your partner. So don't get a divorce if you're both Christians.

   By the way, this is commanded by the Lord, according to verse 10. It's not just a suggestion, just a counselor's nice idea, or just good advice—it's a command! Stay married. Now, he's not considering the adultery exception here. That was considered in Matthew 5 and Matthew 19. Paul doesn't change that; it just isn't brought up here. If there was adultery going on, then there would be freedom to divorce and remarry. But apart from that, Paul reaffirms the divine ideal here and says, "Don't get a divorce. If you do, you'll have to remain formerly married for life or else go back to your partner. That's all you can do."

   If you divorce a Christian partner for reasons other than adultery and then marry somebody else, you become an adulterer, and you turn the person you marry into an adulterer. That's exactly what the Jews were doing. Without legitimate grounds for divorce, they were shedding their wives, remarrying, and committing adultery all over the place.

So if you're married to a Christian—stay married. If you violate that, for God's sake stop there and don't go any further. Get reconciled or else stay single the rest of your life. It seems to me that if two people have only those two options, they're going to be in a hurry to be reconciled—not to remain formerly married.

2. A Christian married to a non-Christian (vv. 12–16)

Let's go to verse 12. Now here are some people who are in mixed marriages, Christian/non-Christian, and the Christians are asking the question, "Should I get out of this union?" The woman, let's say, is married to a guy who worships idols, cheats in his business, and whose language is filthy. This guy is just a typical pagan. Well, all of a sudden Christ transforms and changes her life, and she becomes white as snow and as pure as wool. And as she begins to see all the ugliness of her past and her husband's present sinfulness, she wants to be with God's people. Tertullian wrote about heathen husbands being angry with their Christian wives because they wanted to kiss martyrs' bonds, embrace Christian brothers and sisters, and go along the streets to the cottages of the poor to meet their needs. Many husbands didn't know what was going on. Consequently, it threw them for a loop, and they couldn't handle it.

What do you do? Do you just unload the guy and marry a nice Christian and get on with raising Christian kids? That would seem reasonable, wouldn't it? The Christians probably thought, "I should get rid of the pagan and let him marry another pagan. Then I can marry a Christian and raise a Christian family."

Another question the Christians were asking was, "What's going to happen with all our kids? They're going to be exposed to paganism and will be corrupted by this guy. I mean, all the things that he does will corrupt the whole family. I have to get them out of this deal." Well, that sounds like good counsel, doesn't it? Let's see what Paul says.

a) If the unbeliever wants to stay (vv. 12–14)

(1) Stay together (vv. 12–13)

"But to the rest speak I, not the Lord, If any brother hath a wife that believeth not, and she be pleased to dwell with him, let him not [divorce her]. And the woman who hath an husband that believeth not, and if he be pleased to dwell with her, let her not leave him."

Paul says, "Don't you dare divorce an unbeliever if he doesn't want out. Don't you do that!" You say, "Well, wait a minute. It's going to corrupt me. How can light and darkness go along together? How can Christ and Belial get along? How can you have that kind of relationship—the intimacy of a one-flesh relationship between a believer and an unbeliever? I'd just love to marry a Christian." Paul says, "No, you stay together." You say, "Well, I'm liable to get corrupted, along with all my kids." No, just the opposite's true. Instead of your getting corrupted, the unbeliever's going to get sanctified. Look at verse 14.

(2) Sanctify the family (v. 14)

"For the unbelieving husband is sanctified by the wife, and the unbelieving wife is sanctified by the husband; else were your children unclean, but now are they holy [or 'sanctified']."

Now what kind of sanctification is this? Is this salvation? Do you get saved by having a Christian spouse? Do you get saved by having a Christian mother or father? Of course not. This simply means that the family is set apart unto blessing. In other words, instead of an unbeliever's defiling a home, a believer living with an unbeliever brings blessing into that home. Why? Because as God is pouring out His grace, His benediction, His mercy, His loving-kindness, His goodness, and His blessing on you as a believer, it's going to splash on the person who is one flesh with you. Instead of that person's corrupting you, you're going to bring a positive, Godward influence on that person, and on your children as well.

So don't get a divorce—even if you're married to an unbeliever. Stay together.

b) If the unbeliever divorces (vv. 15–16)

(1) God's call to peace (v. 15)

"But if the unbelieving depart [Gk., chōrizō, 'takes himself out' or 'divorces'], let him depart. A brother or a sister is not under bondage in such cases; but God hath called us to peace."

God hasn't called us to a life of fighting and warring and trying to keep somebody who won't stay. God is not interested in warfare—He's interested in peace. He wants His beloved children to experience peace even in their domestic relationships. So if you're married to an unbeliever who wants to take himself out—let him. You're not in bondage. It is the same idea as in Romans 7:2 where it says a woman is in bondage to her husband only as long as he lives. When he's dead—she's free. It's the same kind of bondage here. When the unbeliever departs—takes himself out of the union—you do not need to fight to keep that marriage together. Why? Because you are no longer under that bondage. God has not called you to live a life of fighting a war with an unbeliever who wants out of his marriage because he can't stand anything about you or what you believe.

Should you compromise your Christian principles to keep your marriage together?

A Christian married to a non-Christian causes all kinds of problems in a family. However, God says, "Stay together unless the unbeliever wants out. Now if that person wants to take himself out, let him." This is a very freeing truth, isn't it? Let me show you something practical about this. You don't have to sacrifice your Christian principles to keep an unbeliever in a marriage. Did you know that? Very often people say to me, "I just have to keep my marriage together. But if I keep doing these spiritual things, it will just irritate him more and more. So if I just acquiesce to his kind of life, we can stay together." Don't do that! Don't you ever compromise God-ordained divine principles! Live those principles out to the very hilt in your life. If your partner has to get out of that marriage because of the purity, sanctity, godliness, and virtue of your life, then the Bible says you're free. But as soon as you start to compromise your spirituality, you're stepping into a never-never land. Why? Because you're going to try to keep a marriage together by violating God's principles. A fighting, quarrelsome home is not God's will—neither is a compromising Christian. Live your life for the glory of God, and do all you can—lovingly, generously, and graciously—to win that partner to Christ.

First Peter 3 says, if you're a wife, to do everything you can to win that one who does not obey the Word, by the purity of your life and your chaste conduct. You be as godly, and as virtuous, and as loving as you can be—but don't you ever compromise your spiritual principles. And if you're a husband in the same situation, you be as loving, and as tender, and as gracious as you can be—but don't you ever abandon the God-given truth, principles, and place of responsibility that you have in that relationship. If that unbelieving partner will not respond to the blessing of God and be led to salvation, but instead reacts in violence to break up the union, then you're free.

(2) God's caution against marital evangelism (v. 16)

"For what knowest thou, O wife, whether thou shalt save thy husband? Or how knowest thou, O man, whether thou shalt save thy wife?"

Someone will invariably say, "If I don't keep my marriage together, who's going to reach my unsaved spouse?" Well, don't try to keep a marriage together for evangelism. Evangelism isn't a good reason to be married. I've heard guys say, "Oh, there's a beautiful girl, I think I'd like to evangelize her. She's not a Christian, but I'll win

93

her to the Lord." Don't you do that. Marriage is not for
evangelism. And evangelism isn't a good reason to keep
one together either.

Why would you spend your whole life fighting and
warring in a marriage where the other person wants out,
just for the sake of an evangelism you don't even know
you can accomplish? Just remember this. The Lord knows
what He's doing. If He's going to minister in that person's heart and bring about the work of grace in that life,
you're not the only person in the world He can use.

So cling to your marriage if you're a believer married to another
believer. Don't divorce. If you're a believer married to an unbeliever, cling to that marriage too. And be everything you should be
as a Christian—living your Christian life to the very fullest. If that
unbeliever wants out, you're free—free to remarry. Now, if that
wasn't true, Paul would have simply repeated what he said in verse
11: "If you divorce, you must remain unmarried or be reconciled."
No, if you're free, you're free—the same freedom that death gives
(Rom. 7:2–3). So if an unbeliever has left you because he wanted
out of that union, you're free.

Now the sum of all that Paul's been saying thus far can be verbalized in
the following question.

IV. SHOULD SALVATION CHANGE YOUR MARITAL STATUS? (vv.
17–24)

A. The Answer Stated (v. 17)

"But as God hath distributed to every man, as the Lord hath called
every one, so let him walk. And so ordain I in all churches."

What is Paul's practical message to the church? His message is this,
"The way God made you, ordained you, and called you, that's the
way you ought to walk." In other words, if He designed you for
marriage, you ought to get married. If He designed you for singleness, you ought to be single. If you were saved married, stay
married. And if you were saved single, stay single—unless you feel
you need to get married. He's just saying, "Look, what I say in all
the churches is that the Lord has to work this out as He distributes
to every individual. And only you and God know whether you need
to be single or married. However, salvation shouldn't change those
things."

B. The Answer Specified (vv. 18–23)

"Is any man called being circumcised? Let him not become uncir-
cumcised. Is any called in uncircumcision? Let him not be circumcised. Circumcision is nothing, and uncircumcision is nothing, but
the keeping of the commandments of God. Let every man abide in
the same calling in which he was called. Art thou called, being a
servant? Care not for it; but if thou mayest be made free, use it

94

rather. For he that is called in the Lord, being a servant, is the Lord's freeman; likewise also he that is called, being free, is Christ's servant. Ye are bought with a price; be not ye the servants of men."

In other words, Paul says, "Whatever state you were in when you were called to the Savior—stay there!"

C. The Answer Summarized (v. 24)

"Brethren, let every man, in whatever state he is called, there abide with God."

So salvation shouldn't tear marriages apart or disrupt life.

Is sex unspiritual? No. Can widowed or divorced people remarry after they become saved? Yes, if they can't stay single for the service of the Lord. What are the alternatives for those who are married when they become Christians? If you're married to a Christian, stay married. If you're married to a non-Christian, stay married—unless the non-Christian wants out—then you're free to remarry. Should salvation change your marital status? No.

Let's look, now, at question number five.

V. SHOULD THOSE THAT HAVE NEVER BEEN MARRIED, MARRY? (vv. 25–35)

A. The Question's Background

The single people in the Corinthian church that had never been married were saying, "Since sex is so evil in our society, now that we want to live pure unto God, we ought to stay celibate for the rest of our lives." Well, the Catholic church still believes that, don't they? They believe there's more virtue in being a celibate than in being married. If you choose to be a priest or a nun, you choose a life of celibacy. So there were some people in the Corinthian church who were saying, "You know, we're virgins. We've never entered into any kind of a sexual relationship. Is it better to stay that way, or should we marry?"

B. The Question's Answer

1. Paul's reaffirmation to stay single (vv. 25, 26b)

"Now concerning virgins [Gk., *parthenoi*], I have no commandment of the Lord; yet I give my judgment, as one that hath obtained mercy of the Lord to be faithful. . . . it is good for a man so to be."

He's right back to the advocating of singleness again, isn't he? You see, society wants to pressure everybody to be married. But there's a reverse trend in this chapter. Paul's trying to pressure people to stay single if they can handle it. Why? Because of the tremendous liberty in serving the Lord. So Paul says, "I think it's good. Stay single."

2. Paul's reasons to stay single (vv. 26, 28–35)

    a) The pressure of the system (v. 26)

"I suppose, therefore, that this is good for the present distress, I say, that it is good for a man so to be."

You say, "The present distress? What is Paul talking about?" He's talking about violence from a hostile world. You know, the time came when Christians were slaughtered everywhere and people lost their partners. There's a lot of pain and anxiety during persecution, isn't there? During the Holocaust in Germany many Jews had their entire families slaughtered. They certainly experienced a tremendous amount of pain. So Paul says, "Because of the violence against us in these times, you'd be better off to be single."

    b) The problems of the flesh (v. 28)

"But and if thou marry, thou hast not sinned; and if a virgin marry, she hath not sinned. Nevertheless, such shall have trouble in the flesh; but I spare you."

It's tough enough for one sinner to live with himself. But for one sinner to live with himself and another sinner is really tough. The flesh constantly gets in the way of our relationships. By the way, the word there for "trouble" is *thlipsis*. It means "the crushing together." When you crush two lives together you're going to have some problems.

    c) The passing of the world (vv. 29–31)

"Time is short," Paul says in verse 29. Then at the end of verse 31 he says, "the fashion of this world passeth away." Everything in the world is going to go anyway, and marriage is part of it. There's no marriage in heaven. So realize it's temporal, passing, just for here and now.

    d) The preoccupation of the married (vv. 32–35)

Married people care for the things of their family—their spouse, their children, and everything else that goes with being married. Unmarried people care for the things of the Lord. So realize this: You're going to be preoccupied in marriage in ways you wouldn't be if you were single.

    e) The permanence of the union

After hearing Jesus teach on the subject of marriage and divorce in Matthew 19, the disciples said, "If marriage is so binding, it's better not to get married." In other words, "Once you get in it, you're in it for life—so you'd better think about it."

Now, let's back up and look at the summary in verses 27–28*a:* "Art thou bound unto a wife? Seek not to be loosed [or 'divorced']. Art thou loosed [or 'divorced'] from a wife? Seek not a wife. But and if thou marry, thou hast not sinned; and if a virgin marry, she hath not sinned." Notice here that two people are given the right to marry, a virgin and a person loosed from a wife—divorced, of course, on divine terms. If you've been loosed from a wife, see if God would have you single. But if you marry, you haven't sinned.

VI. SHOULD FATHERS SPARE THEIR DAUGHTERS THE DIFFICULTIES OF MARRIAGE AND KEEP THEM VIRGINS FOR LIFE? (vv. 36–38)

A. The Question's Background

Do you know what else happened in the Corinthian church? Since they saw sex as evil and celibacy as spiritual, some fathers were imposing perpetual virginity on their daughters. So Paul deals with it in verses 36–38.

B. The Question's Answer

Paul says, "But if any man think that he behaveth himself unseemly toward his virgin [daughter], if she pass the flower of her age [the time of her sexual maturity], and need so require, let him do what he will, he sinneth not; let them marry." Here was a father saying, "Boy, celibacy for the glory of God, and devoting one's whole life to Jesus Christ. I'm going to have my daughter live that kind of spiritual life." However, when she reached the flowering of her age, she said, "Daddy, that's a wonderful thought, but I need to be married." When he insisted that she be spiritual, she said, "But Daddy! I can't be spiritual if I have to be single the rest of my life!" Since it's too difficult a temptation, and her need required her to marry, Paul said, "Hey, Dad, let the girl marry—it's OK."

In verse 38, Paul says, "So, then, he that giveth her in marriage doeth well; but he that giveth her not in marriage doeth better." In other words, "Some of them ought to stay single!"

VII. SHOULD WIDOWS REMARRY? (vv. 39–40)

What about the widows? Should they remarry? Look at verses 39–40: "The wife is bound by the law as long as her husband liveth; but if her husband be dead, she is at liberty to be married to whom she will." And what's the last line again? "Only in the Lord."

Then Paul throws this in: "But she is happier if she so abide." In other words, "She will be happier if she stays the way I am—single!" See, he always has to get that in there. Then he says, at the end of verse 40, "The things I've been saying, I have received from the Holy Spirit."

Conclusion

A. Those That Are Single

If you're single, you fall into one of four categories.

1. By delay

If you're single and you know you're not going to stay that way, what does the Word say to you? Get married, right? It's better to marry than to burn.

97

2. By divine design

If you're single by divine design for the service of Christ, what should you do? Stay single.

3. By divorce

If you're single by divorce, what should you do? Well, first of all, you should consider whether you ought to stay single. Then, if you've been divorced out of an adulterous situation, or if your divorce was before you were saved, or if your divorce was an unbeliever departing—you're free to remarry. In fact, it's also better for you to marry than to burn.

4. By death

The fourth category of singleness is those that are single by death. Stay single if you can. But if you can't, get married—you haven't sinned.

B. Those That Are Married

1. To a Christian

If you're married to a Christian, stay married.

2. To a non-Christian

If you're married to a non-Christian, stay married. However, if the unsaved person wants out—let him out, you're free.

C. Those That Are Illegitimately Divorced and Remarried

Now, there is only one other category. Some of you are saying, "I have a problem. I fouled up my marriage when I was a Christian and got a divorce that wasn't legitimate. Furthermore, I am an adulterer (or an adulteress), because I remarried when I had no grounds. What is my status?" Well, you're a sinner—welcome to the club. If you've already violated God's laws as a Christian and you were illegitimately divorced and remarried (in other words, you're in a union that the Bible defines as an adulterous union), you have only one recourse—to confess the sin, tell God the sorrow of your heart, and stay in that same union. See if God will not make sweet out of the bitter—honey out of the lion's body.

First John 1:9 says, "If we confess our sins, he is faithful and just to forgive us our sins, and to cleanse us from all unrighteousness." It's easy for us who haven't sinned in that area to sit in judgment on those who have, because we forget the sins of our own lives. Well, God's in the sin-forgiving business, isn't He? Matthew 12:31a says, "All manner of sin and blasphemy shall be forgiven men."

Some have suggested that if you're illegitimately divorced and remarried, you have to divorce your present adulterous partner (whom you have made into an adulterer or adulteress) and try to get back with your previous partner. Don't do that! You cannot un-scramble the egg. Stay where you are, confess it, repent of it, and thank God for the grace that you're still alive. Then make the most out of the union you have.

I don't think the Bible is that fuzzy on the issue of divorce. It's pretty clear, isn't it? It's only a question of whether we'll be obedient.

Focusing on the Facts

1. Is Jesus' teaching on divorce applicable only to His day and irrelevant to ours? Explain (see p. 83).

2. Even though Jesus' teaching on divorce in Matthew 19 is very clear, why must we also study Paul's commentary on Jesus' teaching? Where is Paul's commentary found (see p. 84)?

3. How was Paul's audience in 1 Corinthians 7 different from Jesus' audience in Matthew 19? Which one was closer to our own society (see p. 84)?

4. What question did Paul answer in 1 Corinthians 7:1–7? What was his answer (see pp. 84–85)?

5. What are the three categories of singleness referred to in 1 Corinthians 7? Define each one (see pp. 85–86).

6. Why must the term "unmarried" in verse 8 refer to people who have been divorced (see pp. 86–87)?

7. According to Paul, should a formerly married person remarry? Explain (see p. 87).

8. If a formerly married person is not gifted to be single, why is it better to marry (see p. 87)?

9. What's wrong with the statement, "It doesn't matter if your illegitimate divorce occurred before you became a Christian. You're stuck with that mistake for the rest of your life" (see p. 87)?

10. What does Paul mean when he says that a widow is to remarry "only in the Lord" (v. 39b; see p. 88)?

11. If you know you're not gifted to be single for the glory of God, what practical steps can you take to remain pure until God brings about marriage in your life (see pp. 88–89)?

12. How do we know that Paul, in verses 10–11, is speaking to the issue of two Christians divorcing for other than biblical grounds? What is the command that is given concerning this issue (see pp. 89–90)?

13. What options does Paul give to a Christian who divorces another Christian for reasons other than adultery? What is the intent of these options (see pp. 90–91)?

14. Read verses 12–16. Who are "the rest" of verse 12 (see p. 91)?

15. Why would a Christian married to a non-Christian cause problems in a marriage (see p. 91)?

16. Can a Christian who is married to an unbeliever get a divorce on the grounds that they are unequally yoked (2 Cor. 6:17) even though the unbeliever wants to stay married (see pp. 91–92)?

17. Does the unbeliever corrupt the believer in a mixed marriage? Why or why not (see p. 92)?

18. In what way is an unbelieving husband or wife sanctified by a Christian partner (see p. 92)?

19. Should a Christian fight to keep a marriage together with an unbeliever, even if the unbeliever wants out? Why (see pp. 92–93)?

20. Should Christians downplay or compromise their Christian principles in order to pacify an unbelieving partner and keep peace in the home (see p. 93)?

21. Some Christians believe that they must stay married to their unbelieving partner, whatever the cost, in order to bring them to the Lord. What's wrong with this concept of marital evangelism (see pp. 93–94)?

22. Should salvation change one's marital status? Why? How does Paul illustrate this point (see pp. 94–95)?

23. Does a celibate have a higher degree of spirituality? Explain (see pp. 95–96).

24. According to verses 26–35, why does Paul advocate staying single, if at all possible (see pp. 95–96)?

25. What question does Paul answer in verses 36–38? What is his answer (see p. 97)?

26. Does Paul believe that widows will be happier if they remarry or if they stay single (see p. 97)?

27. If you are single, you fall into one of four categories of singleness. What are they? What is the proper response of someone in each category toward marriage (see pp. 97–98)?

28. If you illegitimately divorced and remarried since you became a Christian, what are you to do about the union you're presently in? What is your responsibility towards God (see p. 98)?

Pondering the Principles

1. The eight principles on pages 88–89 on how to handle the pressures of singleness deserve some more attention. If you're single, memorize these principles and ask God to help you implement them in your life. If you're married, share these principles with a single person you know who is struggling with singleness.

2. A common teaching in Christianity today is that remarriage for a divorced person is never permitted. Based on the principles of this chapter, how would you refute this teaching? Do you know someone who is divorced and biblically eligible to remarry, yet is struggling with being single because he has been taught that he can't remarry? Commit yourself to share the principles you've learned in this chapter with that person.

3. Christians who have never had a problem in the area of divorce and remarriage sometimes look down with a condescending attitude on those Christians who have. If you have a tendency to do that, realize that your attitude is sin, confess it to God, and confess it to the person(s) you've looked down on. Have you ever been the recipient of judgmental atti-

tudes from Christians when they found out you were divorced? What was your response? If you've held any grudges or bitterness against another brother or sister in Christ because of his response to your divorce, confess it to the Lord, and then confess it to the individual.

4. Take out a separate piece of paper and write down all the new principles that you have learned from this study. Now share these principles with your spouse and one other person—preferably someone who needs God's solution to his marital problems.

Scripture Index

Moody Press, a ministry of the Moody Bible Institute, is designed for education, evangelization, and edification. If we may assist you in knowing more about Christ and the Christian life, please write us without obligation: Moody Press, % MLM, Chicago, Illinois 60610.